The Little Book of
Darts

Brian Belton

First published 2011

The History Press
The Mill, Brimscombe Port
Stroud, Gloucestershire, GL5 2QG
www.thehistorypress.co.uk

British Library Cataloguing in Publication Data.
A catalogue record for this book is available from the British Library.

ISBN 978 0 7524 6043 7

Typesetting and origination by The History Press
Printed in Great Britain

CONTENTS

FOREWORD
by Bobby George

D arts is an old game; perhaps, in its different incarnations, the oldest. It is so old no one knows when or where it started, let alone why. It's something people play for enjoyment, social interaction or a challenge, and some even look to achieve fame and fortune in a space of 7ft 9¼in.

There is hardly a place on earth where someone at sometime has not played darts. Cities, mountain peaks, deserts, jungles, and at both poles, people have taken time out to throw darts at a board. 3,000-year-old darts have been found in the Egyptian pyramids. In the First World War the solid wooden dartboards of the day were taken to the trenches, something of home, whether you were a Londoner, a Yorkshireman, Scotsman, Welshman, Australian, Jamaican, Indian or German. If ever you see a photograph or a painting of Second World War Spitfire pilots waiting to face the great dark clouds of the invading Luftwaffe, it is likely that somewhere in the scene will be a Nodor Original Bristle Dartboard. As such, darts is part of us, our society and civilisation; where we have been, so have our darts and our boards. One day there'll be darts played on the moon and Mars and people will feel much the same about it as they do here and now or a hundred years ago.

This being the case, Brian Belton's book is a timely addition to the world of darts. It covers every facet of the game, the characters and statistics that are the ticks and tocks of the oche, but there is also history and insight into the razzmatazz of the sport, with all the humour, pathos, amazement, disappointment and glory that comes with it.

Like me, Brian is an East Londoner and from the dockside borough of Newham. He is a life-long fan, follower, supporter and historian of darts, and a fourth-generation player of the game since his boyhood. In this little book he puts the passion and daftness, the pain and the triumph, the commitment and discipline of darts on show, demonstrating how it, maybe more than any other game, reflects what we are as human beings; funny, wonderful, thoughtful, brash, greedy, giving, driven, vulnerable and sometimes a little bit mad. *The Little Book of Darts*, like the game it is about, will cause you to laugh, wonder, remember and perhaps take a second look. It will add to the enjoyment of the next and every other game of darts you play or watch. This is what makes it a must-read for all of us who have been touched and inspired by the flight, thud and fun of what is the sport most clearly connected to the soul and spirit of the common man.

Bobby George, 2011

INTRODUCTION

What is darts? Darts is thundering music, lights flashing, scantily dressed young women gyrating in front of a great horde of excited and celebratory fans. Darts is dressing up as super heroes, Apache warriors, Buzz Lightyear, convicts, schoolgirls, French maids, cows, rhinos, nurses and nuns. Darts is fantasy in real time; it is a game but it is also a world of its own; a place to be who you are and whoever you want to be or never dreamt you'd be.

The crowd jumps and roars, yells and screams. They are armed with cardboard placards that they raise and wave as one ocean of recognition after three darts 'tump, tump, tump' into that tiny letterbox which is the treble 20. Television lights boil the stage in the hottest of hot illumination, denying the winter night that drapes itself outside the doors of this 'house of fun'. Darts is not just darts but a great night out and the knowledge that you might get to see yourself on telly later makes you part of the entertainment.

The audience leap out of a space of festivity and merry bias, diluted by an apparently bottomless well of beer, consumed by the 4-pint jug, fuelled by an endless supply of chips and burgers. Although you can get 3D darts, this is a 5D experience, you can touch it, you can smell it, you can actually be in it. It is this that has caused the fanbase of darts to grow massively in recent times. This is why a tournament winner can walk away with the best part of a quarter of a million quid. But they will also be lauded like an affable pharaoh, not only by the traditional 'life-blood' supporters of the game, from the teeming working-class communities of Britain, but also by the lawyers, showbiz types, professional sports people, bankers and accountants who occupy the £200 corporate hospitality seats. Royalty and celebrities like Stephen Fry, the former England cricketer Andrew Flintoff and retired footballer and radio pundit Robbie Savage, will be proud and excited to call the greatest darters 'friend'.

Compared even to a few years ago it is noticeable that there are more women in darts crowds now and, overall, people are younger (or look younger to me perhaps). The live game's supporters seem to be able to enjoy themselves without trouble. Yes people cheer their favourite players, boo who they see as the 'bad guys', and there is non-stop banter, but unlike many other sports, darts is not tribal; darts supporters are a single clan.

But while the game is about the communal it is also about the individual. All dart players have their own darts stories, for most of us this is more about the social side of the sport than actually playing. Really that is what makes darts the massive phenomenon it is today; it is very much the 'people's game', it is part of our lives and therefore something that's literally lived.

My personal story of the game goes back generations. My great grandfather, Jimmy Stone, and his cousin Sammy played together from childhood up to the First World War. For them, from their teenage years onwards, darts was a raw professional sport, laced with wagers and poker-like pots. Somewhere between Plunkett and Macleane and

Butch Cassidy and the Sundance Kid, Jimmy and Sammy fought out their darts encounters in the back rooms of backstreet pubs, in factories after work or in disused warehouses. They once played in the smoke-filled board room of West Ham United, pitted against a group of professional footballers who were members of the West Ham team, watched and wagered on by the directors of the club. Another time the pair played the best of 101 games in a circus tent pitched on open ground on the edge of London's East End, meeting clowns, the ring master, acrobats and a lion tamer all dressed in their show regalia.

Sammy, a veteran of the Boer War, was around 35 when he said goodbye to his playing partner. Sadly, Jimmy was never to return from the fields of France. However, Sammy, then a slater by trade, continued to play and in 1928, representing the South West Ham Working Men's Club, he became the first winner of the News of the World Championship – the darts World Cup of its day.

My grandfather met my grandmother at a darts match. He was a mean pub player and guess what – his son, my Dad, met my Mum while in a pub, in Poplar, deep in London's Docklands, after a game of darts. As a reluctant conscript soldier, Dad had kept himself in cigarettes by way of darts while serving King and Country in some of the furthest-flung military outposts in Britain. However, it wasn't a bad academy as he went on to distinguish himself as a multi-holiday camp champ right through the 1960s and '70s (we had a cabinet full of the tackiest trophies you can imagine). It wasn't unusual for him to defeat me or my grandfather in the final and semi-finals of these surprisingly ferocious competitions, but sometimes we got the better of him. When beaten by my grandfather he would often smile and mutter, 'Slain by the Maharishi', a epithet that hardly fitted the hulking, toothless, flannel-shirted, steel toecap boot-wearing, city-scarred, barbarian-like, gasworks stoker his father was.

As such, and while I can't say I'm the player Jimmy and Sammy were, I can say darts is in my blood and it is that which has brought the following pages into the world. So this is not really just another book on darts. I think that in these days, when every fact and figure about most of the top players and tournaments is recorded and repeated over and over again in the great clouds of cyberspace, it is not enough merely to reproduce recent tournament outcomes and the potted life stories of contemporary stars. That said, some of that is unavoidable if one is to provide even a decent snapshot of darts as a sport. But in what follows I hope you will find something of the character and spirit of the game; its presence in the world as a great cavalcade of excitement, competition and fun.

I have not tried to write a darts history; the scholarly work of the peerless Patrick Chaplin on his website (www.patrickchaplin.com) and his book, *Darts in England* (2009), is the benchmark of such a pursuit, and I, like anyone interested in the chronicles of darts, owe a debt to his endeavour and need to acknowledge his supremacy in this realm; I thank him for his precise and honest efforts to provide the sport with the distinction of rigorous historical research. In this book I've made an effort to offer something of a tour round darts, perhaps taking the reader down a few of the less well-travelled byways of the game.

I have played darts in Shanghai, Hong Kong, Uruguay and Argentina. As a nine-year-old, during an afternoon 'lock-in', I partnered my father in a doubles game at the Retreat Pub in Essex against Bobby Moore and his fellow England soccer international Johnny 'Budgie' Byrne (they had been on the sherbets most of the day as I recall). I have walked towards oches on the Falkland Islands, in

Malaysia, Zambia and Slovenia. I've played Frenchmen in Germany, Danes in Iceland, Namibians in Cuba, Germans in Holland and Arabs in Spain; in 1972, in Berlin I found myself throwing against an Italian transvestite called 'Bilbo' and a drunken Ukrainian who answered to the name of 'Fido' (at least that evening). For a while I travelled, as a sort of privateer player, right down the west coast of the USA, throwing for fun, hope and dollars as I buttered my bread via casual work between milking and being milked by the greyhound and trotting racetracks of that part of the world. In the process of all this I've picked up thousands of stories about darts and darters. Plenty sounded like illusions, others were incredible, a few were insane, others were mundane, commonly they were inane. I've listened to different versions, variations and lots of assimilations of these often anecdotal, frequently narrative, sometimes symbolic stories. I have also, since I was a kid, on dark nights, cold days and sunny beaches, over breakfast and dinner tables, in hop fields and from bedside chairs and hospital beds, been told darting family tales. I have included a few of these myths, legends and apocryphal parables in this little collection of darts life, this journey through the world that by picking up this book I know that we, at least to some extent, share. I hope, as I hope my next dart is a double or a top treble, that you enjoy them and all the facts, figures, memories, nostalgia, inspiring words, the enigma and the bits of fun brought together in this cosy package.

Unlike many other professional, world sports, darts has retained its humanity, its connection with people and it is that 'realness' which you will identify with and maybe celebrate in this little book, this big world of darts.

Shall we diddle?

Brian Belton, 2011

FOR THE RECORD

In May 1987, Duncan Swift, of the Felixstowe Dock Sports and Social Club (now the the Trimley Sports & Social Club in Suffolk), scored 493,470 to claim the 24-hour solo darts record. Throwing and retrieving the darts himself, Swift got a total of 123 180s and 643 140s. He slung 18,369 darts, clocking a 26.86-point average per dart.

HERO

Darts has its heroes and its villains; players who fans love to hate and those they take to their hearts. The categorisation will change from person to person, but there are some professionals who seem to inspire these particular feelings more than others.

At the age of 18 Adrian Lewis won the 2003 British Teenage Open. Two years later, in the UK Open, his 11–0 whitewash of Colin Monk, to make the last 16, was one of the few in the tournament's history. Adrian's continued success since this time makes it difficult not to admire him and he is sowing the seeds of making himself a legend of the game.

This said, he has looked temperamental at times. During his 2006 debut in the World Championship, Lewis left the stage before the end of his quarter-final clash with Peter Manley, alleging Manley had been attempting to upset him while he was throwing.

In the first round of the 2008 European Darts Championship, Adrian encountered Hannes Schnier. He came on stage with three plasters on his non-throwing hand after trying to catch a falling glass backstage which had shattered in his hand. Despite needing hospital treatment for two deep cuts, Lewis got to the final only to be beaten 11–5 by Phil Taylor.

In the 2009 World Grand Prix, Lewis exchanged words with Gary Anderson as the latter felt Lewis went into the exclusion zone while he was throwing. Lewis appeared to be unfazed as he won the match 3–2.

Adrian's first televised final on Sky was the 2010 World Grand Prix. He defeated Phil Taylor for the first time on television in the semi-finals but, with Taylor accusing Lewis of playing up to the crowd to put him off, the move into the final was just a little sour. In the final the next day, the tables were turned somewhat with Lewis claiming that James Wade had put him off his throw by allegedly 'stamping' on the oche.

In 2011 Lewis met Gary Anderson in the PDC World Championship final. During the first set, Lewis became the first player to throw a nine-dart finish in a World Championship final. He won the match 7–5.

Getting off to a winning start in the 2011 Premier League, Lewis annihilated the 2010 champion Phil Taylor 8–2 – Taylor's biggest defeat in the history of the tournament. Adrian went on to meet Gary Anderson in Glasgow. Lewis was booed and coins were thrown at him, but he went on to beat the Flying Scotsman 8–3 after being 3–0 down. Lewis made it to the final but lost 10–4 to Anderson.

Lewis has been known to hit 'blind' shots during matches, most notably during 180 attempts. Recordings show him hitting a 180 without looking against Peter

Manley and repeatedly failing to do so against Raymond van Barneveld.

At the time of writing Lewis has won close to £900,000 during his five-year career.

A TO Z OF PLAYER NICKNAMES

Martin Adams	Wolfie
Steve Alker	The Snake Man
Bob Anderson	The Limestone Cowboy
Gary Anderson	Dreamboy or The Flying Scotsman
Irena Armstrong	Ice Baby
Dave Askew	Diamond Dave
Martin Atkins	The Assassin

SUPER, SMASHING, GREAT

Bullseye was a hugely popular, darts-based television quiz show that was first created for the ITV network by ATV in 1981. It was then made by Central from 1982 until 1995, and hosted by club comedian Jim Bowen. Originally aired on Monday nights, from the second series starting in 1982 up to 1993 it went out on Sunday evenings, pulling in an audience of approximately 17 million. Thereafter it took a Saturday afternoon slot.

The programme involved three pairs of contestants (one person in each team would answer questions, the other was designated to throw darts). The teams would be pitted against one another over three rounds with the victorious pair gaining the chance to win a holiday, a car, domestic equipment or even (joy of joys) a speedboat. Losing contestants would go away with of a set of commemorative darts, a tankard (or a silver goblet for the ladies) and a 'Bendy Bully' – which is what they really came for.

From the second series, with Tony Green the darts commentator co-hosting the show, *Bullseye* began to become something of an institution of the winter months. The 'everyman' approach of former deputy headmaster Bowen (real name Peter Williams) and catchphrases became part of television vernacular. In the show's heyday I was a youth worker in East London and Cockney kids, on being berated for some misdemeanour, would respond in a well-rehearsed mimic of Bowen's Lancashire accent, 'Super, smashing, great'; at which it was hard not to smile. Or after scoring a goal in football, or escape paying subscriptions (yet again) cry out, as if in praise of Tony Green, 'One hundred and eiiiiiightyyyyyy!'

In 2005, Andrew Wood, the creator of *Bullseye* (it seems comedian Norman Vaughan also had a hand in the development of the show) declared that he had signed a contract with Granada Media for them to produce an hour-long celebrity special *Bullseye* that Ant and Dec would host as part of the *Gameshow Marathon* they were undertaking in connection with ITV's 50th anniversary celebrations. The show went out on ITV on 22 October 2005. Vernon Kay and *Coronation Street* star William Roache were the contestants, attended by Eric Bristow and Andy Fordham. Tony Green returned as co-host.

Subsequently Granada decided that a new series of *Bullseye* would be produced early the following year by Yorkshire Television at their Leeds studios. On 25 January 2006, it was proclaimed that satellite channel

Challenge had won the rights to show the new series. So *Bullseye* returned to our screens on Challenge at 10.00 p.m. on 17 April 2006. The show maintained the same type of prizes as the original format – none of the cash prizes had increased in value since the first show. In the name of progress, some of the prizes featured on Bully's Prize Board were a bit more up to date than the goodies which used to appear on the ITV show. No more Goblin teasmades and beige toasters . . .

YOU CAN'T BEAT A BIT OF BULLY

Dave Spikey and Tony Green appeared on the Colin and Edith show on Radio 1 in 2006 and remembered the original *Bullseye* as 'The only game show on the television in which the prizes get a round of applause.' But though I jest, the prizes on *Bullseye* were more than respectable for the show's time. You could win cars and holidays if you were lucky – however, should contestants lose the gamble, they had to see the star prize regardless; the 'look at what you could have won' moment was quite sadistic really.

Contestants were given the option of gambling all the money and prizes they had won on the show against winning the star prize. If they took the gamble they would need to score 101 or more with six darts to win. The non-dart player would throw first, followed by the dart player. Scoring 101 not only got them the star prize, but they also got to keep all of the other prizes and cash they had won earlier. If they failed to score 101 or more, they lost everything, but as Bowen always said, 'yer charity money's safe!'

SOMETHING TO PLAY FOR

The News of the World Championship started in 1927 following discussions with the then ruling body, the National Darts Association (NDA). It is uncertain if the NDA or the *News of the World* instigated the idea, but the confirmation that the newspaper was going to sponsor an individual darts contest was initially flagged up in August 1927 in the *Morning Advertiser*. This was followed by corroboration in September of the same year in the *News of the World*.

This was one of the first organised mass darts competitions and for many years the only major darts contest that the ordinary player might win. For most of the third quarter of the twentieth century, the News of the World Championship became the central dream and hope of darts players. It made darts a truly national pastime and was seminal in the making of the sport we know today.

The *News of the World* provided a 25 guinea trophy (a reproduction of this would be awarded each year to the winning player). Prizes would also be given to beaten finalists. There were no rules about what association or club one was part of (or not). Entry was free through a local pub and matches were contested within manageable travelling distance of that pub. However, the competition's initial aim was fairly modest – to establish who was the top darts player in the metropolitan police area.

In pubs, works canteens and social clubs, the beginning of the season would see the organisation of 'house' tournaments. The victors of these events would receive certificates proclaiming them News of the World 'House Champion'. Certificates were also provided for 180s and throughout the championship silver dart sets were given as a reward for the best weekly performance in the tournament.

On the completion of the 'house' contests, winners were matched in sub-area and area competitions. Each year, the victors from these groupings, together with the publicans, were invited to attend the Grand Finals in London; for darts, and perhaps all so-called pub games, the 'Greatest Show on Earth'.

The format of the competition was the same (three legs, 501, straight start) from the first round in the pubs and clubs to the Grand Finals on stage. Many 'after-work players' found themselves on a regional stage, throwing in front of a crowd of many hundreds or even thousands. It was not unusual for top players to be eliminated by unknowns in early rounds at the Grand Finals. As such, it was the FA Cup of darts and for many who remember it, the likes of the Embassy, the Desert Classic, World Matchplay or World Trophy have been no match for the excitement and romance of the 'News of the World'.

In its first eight years the competition was restricted to the London area. However, over time it grew into the largest darts tournament in world history and the best players of the time took part. The inaugural tournament attracted 1,010 competitors and the first championship final was held on 2 May 1928 at Holborn Hall, Gray's Inn Road, London. The first champion was a forty-nine-year-old slater, father of nine and veteran of the Boer War, Sammy Stone (a cousin of my own great-grandfather, Jimmy Stone). The Championship quickly became to be known as, 'the championship every dart player wants to win', a reputation it carried for the rest of its history.

News of the World Finals: London Area

Year/Winner	Club	Score
1927–28 Sammy Stone	New South-West Ham Club	2–0
1928–29 J. Hoare	Duke's Head, E. Twickenham	2–0
1929–30 C. Bowley	Shakespeare's Head, Finsbury	2–0
1930–31 Tommy Nye	Tankerville Arms, Kennington	2–0
1931–32 Jack Hood	Hood's Dartboards, Bow	2–0
1932–33 Kenny Enever	The Bull, Mitcham	2–1
1933–34 Fred Metson	Hanbury Arms, Islington	2–0
1934–35 Billy Forecast	Duke of York, Bow	2–0

DID YOU KNOW?

From a peak during the 1980s, over the following decade darts saw a huge decline in sponsor interest and it lost most of the television coverage it had previously gained.

Many players felt that the BDO was not doing the sport any favours at its highest level. So, in 1993, a group of players broke away from the game's ruling body and formed their own organisation; the World Darts Council, which was later renamed the Professional Darts Corporation (PDC) that we are more familiar with today.

This being the case, the 1993 World Championship was the last unified event as the BDO refused to allow the new organisation to set up and run its own tournaments. In response to this the WDC players decided that they would no longer compete in the BDO World Championship and founded the World Darts Championship as an alternative.

DUTCH NINE

Raymond van Barneveld hit his first televised nine-dart finish on 23 March 2006 in the International Darts League.

FOR THE RECORD

On 25 November 1985 Alan Powling and Eddie Davies scored 1,000,001 throwing 48,334 darts at Christ the Servant Church, Digmoor, Skelmersdale.

On 12/13 June 1987 eight players of the Jobby Crossan select team from Derry reached 1,000,0001 in 36,750 darts.

VILLAIN

Paul Nicholson is widely known these days as the 'bad boy of darts'. Although British-born, he holds Australian nationality and prior to joining the PDC Pro Tour, Nicholson was one of the top exponents of the game in the Dart Players of Australia (DPA) rankings, having won 15 titles on the Australian circuit in 2008. This earned him a spot in the 2008 Grand Slam of Darts and he caused quite an upset beating Gary Anderson 5–4 in his opening group game. He did this in spite of constant booing from the crowd which had started at his walk-on. Following his first three darts, a maximum 180, he put his finger to his mouth, as if telling the crowd to 'hush'; this provoked the persistent chant of 'Who are ya?' and his every dart was met with boos. The victory over Anderson was not enough to take him out of his group, however, and he was eliminated from the competition.

In the 2009 PDC World Darts Championship Nicholson overwhelmed Adrian Gray in the first round, taking all nine legs for a 3–0 sets win. He then upset the odds by hacking down world number six Adrian Lewis (4–3) and another shock followed – from two sets down Paul came back to sweep aside world number eleven Dennis Priestley (4–2). It took world number three at the time, James Wade, to finish Paul's tournament but his performance slotted him into the top 50 in the PDC Order of Merit.

In the UK Open Paul lost 9–7 to pub qualifier Ken Mather in the third round and afterwards Nicholson's relationship with the crowd dropped to a new low, as he claimed Mather's supporters had consistently shouted out as he was throwing. Provoked by the now-familiar chants of 'Who are ya?', Nicholson responded by swearing at the crowd and was later fined for his outburst by the Darts Regulation Authority.

In 2010, Nicholson claimed his first PDC title, the Totesport Players' Championship, playing the quarter-final, the semi-final and the final in the same day. In the quarters Adrian Lewis was vanquished 9–7. Sensationally Paul defeated reigning champion Phil Taylor 10–9, pushing on to claim a 13–11 title win over Mervyn King. During the last part of the tournament the supporters began to get behind Nicholson, appreciating his efforts against better, more experienced and higher-ranked players. Nicholson's subsequent moderation of his 'bad boy' persona caused some commentators to speculate that Paul might abandon his image as the people's favourite villain of the game.

In 2011 Paul Nicholson won the Crawley Players Championship, defeating Adrian Lewis 6–4 in the final, on the back of a tough fight in the semi with Gary Anderson, in which he pulled through 6–5. In the UK Open of that year Paul defeated Gary Anderson, the Premier League champion, 9–8. The same day Phil Taylor was beaten 9–8, but Paul went down 10–7 to James Wade.

A TO Z OF PLAYER NICKNAMES

Barrie Bates	Champagne or Batesey
Ronnie Baxter	the Rocket, Rocket Ronnie
Steve Beaton	Magnum PI or the Bronzed Adonis
Hans Blijs	the Dominator
Andy Boulton	the 'X' Factor
André Brantjes	the Quiet Man

Eric Bristow	the Crafty Cockney
Stacy Bromberg	the Wish Granter
Steve Brown (Eng)	the Bomber
Steve Brown (USA)	Brownie or the Original
Patrick Bulen	the Pitbull
Stephen Bunting	the Bullet
Martin Burchell	Scarface
Shayne Burgess	Bulldog
Richie Burnett	Prince of Wales

ANYONE FOR A BIT MORE BULLY?

On 14 March 2006 it was announced that the new *Bullseye* was to be hosted by comedian Dave Spikey, who, incidentally, had also appeared as a contestant on the show in the 1980s.

The Bully character received a make-over of sorts for the new series, although most people might have been pushed to notice the 'old Bully' had been ousted by a 'new Bully'.

The reconstituted *Bullseye* was, unlike most other game show revivals in the UK, pretty much the same format as the original series. The original theme tune reappeared, a similar set was used, and the new titles were based on the old ones.

The two new series that were aired in 2006 each consisted of fifteen episodes, but the show has not been produced since then – more's the pity.

DID YOU KNOW?

Peter Manley is married to Crissy Manley (née Howat), who is also a darts player. Peter asked Crissy to marry him after winning the Las Vegas Desert Classic in 2003 and they celebrated their marriage in Las Vegas the following year. Many fellow darts players were in attendance at the wedding, and Wayne Mardle did the honours as Manley's best man.

NINE-DART WONDERS

Raymond van Barneveld threw his second televised nine-dart finish on 2 January 2009 in the quarter-finals of the 2009 PDC World Darts Championship The match was against Jelle Klaasen. Barney hit two maximum 180s before nailing treble 20, treble 19 and double 12 to complete his nine-darter in the second leg of the sixth set.

That nine-darter earned Barneveld £20,000 and he became the first player ever to throw a perfect leg in the PDC World Championship.

Barneveld went on to win the match 5–1, with a three-dart 161 finish, and then won his semi-final against James Wade. Ray was then the only person, apart from Taylor, to have thrown more than one televised perfect leg. Though he progressed to the final, he was beaten by Phil Taylor.

FOR THE RECORD

Stephen Wagg set the 12-hour solo record for scoring double and single bulls at the Thorncliffe Cricket and Social Club in Sheffield in April 1988. He hit 961 double bulls and 3,335 single bulls to make a 131,425 total. In setting the record, Wagg threw a total of 9,714 darts, with a per-dart average of 13.52.

HERO

Phil Taylor is the player most non-darts fans will recognise by name and face. His success, plus his 'everyman' quality, has probably made him the most popular of darts players.

Born in Stoke in 1960, the one-time ceramics worker from Burslem is now recognised as one of the most successful individual sporting champions of all time, having won more than 150 professional tournaments and a record 15 World Championships – a figure unlikely to be surpassed.

He has won the PDC Player of the year four times (2006, 2008, 2009 and 2010) and has been twice nominated for the BBC Sports Personality of the Year award (2006 and 2010). He was the first person to hit two nine-darters in one match (in the 2010 Premier League Darts final against James Wade). To date Phil has achieved nine televised nine-dart finishes, and is ranked World No. 1 in the PDC Order of Merit.

Taylor took up the game seriously fairly late on in his life (in 1986) after moving into a terraced house in Burslem, close to Eric Bristow's pub the Crafty Cockney.

By 1988 Phil had been selected for the county team and he was playing at Super League level. Bristow began sponsoring him, loaning Taylor £10,000 to help him get started as a professional darts player and on the condition that he gave up his job as a ceramic engineer.

Phil's first title was the Canadian Open in 1988. He qualified for the World Championships for the first time in 1990 as a 125-1 unseeded outsider. But he fought his way to the final where he met his mentor, Bristow, then the world number one. Taylor beat Bristow 6–1 and for the rest of 1990 dominated the open events taking titles that included the British Masters, Europe Cup and the game's second most important tournament at the time, the Winmau World Masters.

In 1992 Taylor regained the World Championship, beating Mike Gregory 6–5 in the final, naming that win as the favourite of his career. Rod Harrington reached his first World Final in 1995 but it was Taylor who took the title 6–2.

The finals of 1996, 1997 and 1998 would feature Taylor v Priestley; however Taylor won them all, in doing so passing his mentor Bristow's five World Championships. Phil won the World Matchplay event twice in the first five years of the tournament, beating Priestley 16–11 in 1995 and Alan Warriner-Little 16–11 in 1997.

Taylor stretched his unbeaten run to eight years in the PDC World Championship, beating Peter Manley in 1999 and 2002, Priestley for a fourth time in 2000 and John Part in 2001. Part would finally end this magnificent run by beating Taylor 7–6 in the 2003 tournament. But Phil claimed the World Matchplay title for the next five years (2000–2004) beating five different opponents in the final, Alan Warriner-Little (2000), Richie Burnett (2001), John Part (2002), Wayne Mardle (2003) and Mark Dudbridge

(2004). By the end of 2004, Taylor had won 11 World Championships and seven World Matchplays.

Taylor has faced the incumbent BDO World Champion in challenge matches on two occasions. In 1999 he beat Raymond van Barneveld by 21 legs to 10 in a one-hour challenge dubbed 'The Match of the Century' at the Wembley Conference Centre. The second challenge match came in 2004 against Andy Fordham. Taylor was leading 5–2 in sets when Fordham, feeling unwell, abandoned the match.

Taylor continued to dominate the scene during 2004 and 2005, and won his thirteenth World Championship title in January 2006. Further success in the World Matchplay, the World Darts Trophy (a BDO-affiliated event), and the World Grand Prix followed.

In 2008 Taylor finished at the top of the Premier League standings. He beat Adrian Lewis 11–1 with a 112.68 average in the semi-final, and went on to take his fourth consecutive title with a 16–8 victory over Wade (his average for each trip to the oche was 108.36). He won his second US Open title in May 2008, defeating Colin Lloyd in the final.

In 2008 he regained the World Matchplay, World Grand Prix, won the first European Darts Championship and the Grand Slam of Darts. Taylor won the World Championship title (his fourteenth title) for the first time in three years by beating Raymond van Barneveld 7–1 in the 2009 contest. Taylor beat Colin Osborne 11–6 in the final to win his third UK Open title in June of that year, his first win at this tournament since 2005. His tournament average was 107.38.

Phil's winning streak continued throughout the rest of 2009 with victories in the final Las Vegas Desert Classic (the fifth time he had lifted this title), the World

Matchplay, the World Grand Prix, European Darts Championship and the Grand Slam of Darts for the third successive time in November.

Taylor started 2010 with his fifteenth World Championship title, beating Simon Whitlock 7–3 with an average of more than 104 and winning the match with a 131 checkout. Phil made history again in the Premier League final against defending champion James Wade by hitting two nine-dart finishes, the first time this has been achieved in professional darts.

By the summer of 2010 Phil was the holder of the World Championship, World Matchplay, Premier League, UK Open, World Grand Prix and Grand Slam of Darts – with only the Players' Championship Finals missing from a complete set of major televised titles. These performances, in addition to his longevity, contributed to his nomination for the BBC Sports Personality of the Year award in 2010, where he was voted runner-up to jockey Tony McCoy.

In 2011 he won his first major tournament in seven months by claiming victory in the Players' Championship, beating Gary Anderson 13–12 in a thrilling final.

A TO Z OF PLAYER NICKNAMES

Andy Callaby	Super Cally
Magnus Caris	Poker Face
Roger Carter	Taz
Ray Carver	Razor
Jamie Caven	Jabba
Alan Caves	The Caveman
Jason Clark	the Cockney Jock

Matt Clark	Superman
Erik Clarys	the Sheriff
Mitchell Clegg	the Moosta
Matt Chapman	Baby-Faced Assassin
Dave Chisnall	Chizzy
Steve Coote	Magic

BACK TO BULLY

On 19 May 2007, an hour-long celebrity special of *Bullseye* went out on ITV as part of Vernon Kay's *Gameshow Marathon*. The celebrity contestants were newsreader Andrea Catherwood, former Chelsea footballer Graeme Le Saux and Kevin from *Coronation Street* – Michael Le Vell. They were respectively paired with darts legends Martin Adams, Phil Taylor and Raymond van Barneveld. Tony Green co-hosted the show – it really wouldn't be the same without him.

READ ALL ABOUT IT!

In 1935 the News of the World Championship expanded to take in the Home Counties, an area that has never had an official definition, although the term was used in legislation and the administration of the armed forces throughout the twentieth century. Over the period the championship drew on this area, most people would have taken the region to have included Buckinghamshire, Essex, Hertfordshire, Kent, Surrey, Middlesex and Berkshire. This was clearly a hotbed of talent as during the three years that the championship was limited to this area not a single London-based player won the title and only one, Albert White, made the final.

At this time the *News of the World* had a readership of millions. In 1930–1 it was able to boast 24.32 per cent of the total readership of all the Sunday newspapers; a vast swathe of the working class population. So by mid-decade it is perhaps not surprising that the championship was a massive undertaking and the staff of the *News of the World*, together with hundreds of voluntary organisers (this was Big Society in operation 80 years before Cameron's version of much the same thing), managed what had grown to be a huge organisational task. This characterised the first golden age of darts.

During the years between the wars, the News of the World Championship had a huge role in popularising darts, but it is also important in terms of the history of the game, as by the 1970s, it would grow into an international darts tournament of great renown.

News of the World Finals
London and the Home Counties

Year/Winner	Club	Score
1935–36 Peter Finnigan	Eight Bells, Tolworth	2–0
1936–37 Stan Outten	Seven Kings Hotel, Ilford	2–0
1937–38 Fred Wallis	Railway Hotel, Eastbourne	2–1

In 1936 the competition developed a regional championship format starting in Wales, followed by the first and last Lancashire tournament.

Women were allowed to participate in the News of the World events in open competition against men. This was extraordinary at a time in history when sporting and many other social situations would not countenance open fraternisation between the sexes. However, in practice, mixed competition was mostly confined to southern England.

Although females rarely made the area finals, there is certainly evidence that they could often give good male players a run for their money. For example, in May 1936 Miss E. Turnage, from the Cherry Tree, Cressing Road, Witham, Essex (she was daughter of James Turnage, the licensee of the Cherry Tree), became the first woman to reach the last eight of a News of the World area final. That was held at the Golden Fleece in Chelmsford. The following year, on Monday 12 April, Mrs A. Morgan of the Old House at Home, Golden Common, Hampshire, made it through to Winchester area News of the World Individual Championship, having won four previous rounds, all against men. Mrs Morgan also won the Winchester area competition against an all-male field to become the first woman to win a News of the World area title.

On 24 June Mrs Morgan, the wife of the licensee of the Old House at Home, joined thirty-one other area champions (all men) at the Agricultural Hall, Westminster. She brought a strong crowd of supporters with her. Although Mrs Morgan could not produce her home form, getting herself eliminated in the first round, her performance was never bettered by any woman in the history of the competition.

Towards the end of the decade other national Sunday newspapers were looking to get in on the darts act. The *People*, alongside the NDA, in October 1938, set up a national team contest, while the *Sunday Pictorial* organised a pairs championship, encompassing England, Wales and Scotland. The latter competition also allowed for the participation of women, in that it accepted entries from couples from both genders as well as mixed-gender pairs. Thus darts became a flagship of gender equality in sport! The entry fees for this tournament were donated to the Pirates' Spring Holiday Home for Blind Children, managed by the Royal National Institute for the Blind (RNIB).

News of the World Finals – Wales

Year/Winner	Club	Score
1936–37		
D. Cornacia	Ivy Bush Hotel, Pontardawe	2–0
1937–38		
Gwyn Jones	Unemployed Club, Penygraig	2–0

Lancashire
1937–38		
Sam McIntosh	Duke of York, Salford	2–0

RADIO GAGA

In November 1938 Fred Wallis, the London and Home Counties News of the World winner of 1937–38, took on 'all listeners' in a rather strange radio broadcast from

Eastbourne. In the Alexander Arms Fred threw three darts and this was followed by a pause to allow listeners to throw three darts. This way, the whole audience was able to play Wallis, although what happened if one won is unclear.

DID YOU KNOW?

Raymond van Barneveld is naturally left-handed, but he throws darts with his right hand.

DUTCH NINE

Raymond van Barneveld threw his third nine-dart finish in the Blue Square UK Open West Midlands Regional final on 29 March 2009 in the third round against Kirk Shepherd. His reward for this was just £400 as Mervyn King had claimed the £4,000 bonus on 28 March 2009 at the Coventry Players' Championship with his nine-dart finish.

VILLAIN

Peter Manley, originally from Surrey but now living in Carlisle, had been the Chair of the Professional Dart Players' Association for six years in 2011. However, he is more famous for his long-running and not always friendly rivalry with Phil Taylor. It all stemmed from

Manley's refusal to shake Taylor's hand following his 7–0 drubbing in the 2002 PDC World Championship final. Since then darts fans have made him the target of their derision.

Manley took the Las Vegas Desert Classic in 2003, beating John Part 16–12 in the final. To date that remains his single major PDC tournament win. That said, he has reached the World Championship final three times, though each time Taylor has been his nemesis (twice Peter had to stomach 0–7 thumpings). Manley got the better of Taylor in the semi-final of the 1999 World Matchplay, only to lose 17–19 to Rod Harrington in the final. Peter has been a semi-finalist in the UK Open, World Matchplay and World Grand Prix since then, and qualified for the first four seasons of the Premier League, finishing a creditable third in 2005 with 12 points.

In 2005 Peter changed his entrance music from Chumbawamba's 'Tubthumping' to Tony Christie's 'Is this the way to Amarillo?', which had just topped the UK charts. This gave rise to more positive response from darts fans, although they continue to boo Manley following his musical entrance.

For the most part, Manley is responded to like a pantomime villain rather than with any sincere animosity, but in the quarter finals of 2006 PDC World Championship, his muted words to Adrian Lewis resulted in the latter leaving the stage. It seemed that Manley's response was provoked by Adrian throwing a 'Blind' 180 – he threw the first two darts as normal, hitting two treble 20s, but the last arrow hit home while Lewis was looking back at the crowd and Manley. Although Lewis returned to the game, Manley ended up the winner. For the final, Manley had to endure the vast majority of fans exhibiting their disapproval of his earlier behaviour.

Peter stoked this fire when, during an interview on Sky Sports, he commented that he didn't care what other people thought as he'd made his money (he went away with £50,000 for reaching the final). Manley was beaten in the final 7–0 by Lewis's long time mentor Phil Taylor.

In the 2007 PDC World Championship, Manley exchanged words with Wynand Havenga in the second round, which appeared to be prompted by Havenga's prolonged celebrations after winning a set. On losing the match Peter seemed to apologise, but his gift for contention continued, this time during a match at the Las Vegas Desert Classic, when once more, words were exchanged on stage with Adrian Lewis. Post-match, Manley did his best to give the impression it was a lot of fuss about not much, but Lewis continued to complain after he left the stage.

A TO Z OF PLAYER NICKNAMES

Tony David	The Deadly Boomerang
Ritchie Davies	Lamp Chop
Keith Deller	Milky Bar Kid/The Feller
Brian Derbyshire	Derby
Mieke de Boer	Bambie
Jan Dekker	Mr Cool
Niels de Ruiter	Excellent Dude
Anastasia Dobromyslova	From Russia With Love
Brendan Dolan	Carrontreemall Kid
Mark Dudbridge	The Flash
Steve Duke Snr	Dukey of the Duke

BULLY'S NOTES

The gameshow *Bullseye* was unusual in having two different closing theme tunes – its normal, happy tune was used when the victorious pair won the star prize, and the same tune played in a downbeat manner when they lost or on the rare occasions on which nobody took the gamble.

FOR THE RECORD

An eight-hour record by a two-man team for scoring bulls and outer-ring bulls was set by Birmingham players George Perry and Tony Hodgkiss at the pub the Seventh Trap in December 1987. The pair, with a per-dart average of 16.19, hit 1,406 bulls and 4,247 outer-ring bulls to score 176,475 points, bettering the previous record of 1,048 double bulls and 3,308 single bulls.

HERO

Aldershot-born James Wade became the youngest player ever to win a major PDC title at the World Matchplay in July 2007. Overcoming his earlier 'villain' status, he has since become one of the most popular players in darts.

James won the 2007 World Grand Prix, the 2008 and 2011 UK Opens, the 2009 Premier League, the 2010 World Grand Prix and 2010 Championship League Darts, and, at the time of writing, is at a career-high ranking of second in the PDC Order of Merit. He is officially the second most successful player in PDC history, after Phil Taylor.

Wade reached the final of the British Classic in 2001 at the age of just eighteen, losing to John 'Boy' Walton, but the following year he won the Swiss Open and then made his television debut at the 2003 Lakeside World Championship, although he lost 2–3 in the first round to Dennis Harbour, having missed a staggering eight darts to win the match in the fourth set.

Wade made his PDC World Darts Championship debut in 2005, losing in the first round to Mark Holden. He bounced back from this to win the Irish Masters in February, but he made his major breakthrough on television during the 2006 World Matchplay in July, reaching the final in his first ever appearance at the Winter Gardens, where he met Phil Taylor. At one point he was 8–5 up, but he ended up on the end of 18–11 defeat. For all this, James returned to Blackpool in 2007 to claim the title – his first major televised tournament success and, at the same time, became the youngest player ever to win a PDC televised event, beating Terry Jenkins in the final.

He also won the next PDC major tournament – the 2007 World Grand Prix in Dublin in October, defeating Raymond van Barneveld by 5–1 in the semi-final and repeating his Blackpool success over Jenkins in the final.

James won the 2007 PDC Player of the Year, becoming the second recipient of this award following in the footsteps of Phil Taylor in 2006. In January 2008 Wade became the first player to defeat Phil Taylor in the Premier League, winning the match 8–6.

On 8 June that year, Wade beat American Gary Mawson 11–7 in the final of the UK Open, claiming his third major trophy within a year. He won the 2009

Premier League Darts tournament, defeating Mervyn King 13–8 at Wembley Arena and the 2010 World Grand Prix, beating Adrian Lewis 6–3 in the final. Four days later, he won his second major tournament inside a week by defeating Taylor 6–5 in the 2010 Championship League Darts final.

James became the first player to hit three tournament nine-dart finishes in a calendar year during 2006. They came at the North-West UK Open Regional Final in March, the PDPA Players' Championship at Hayling Island in June and he completed his hat-trick at the Vauxhall Men's Open in November. Unfortunately none of these achievements were in televised competitions.

Wade came within one dart of achieving the first ever nine-darter with a double start at the 2007 World Grand Prix in Dublin. In the semi-final against van Barneveld he hit double top to open the leg, then six treble 20s and treble 17, but then failed to hit the bull and thus missed out on a unique nine-darter.

On 20 November 2008, Wade completed his first live televised nine-darter, hitting two 180s then treble 20, treble 19 and double 12 against Gary Anderson in the second round of the 2008 Grand Slam of Darts, which was shown on ITV4. However, it was Anderson who went on to win the match 10–8, therefore Wade became the first man to hit a nine-dart finish in a major televised tournament in the UK and then to lose the match (although Michael van Gerwen had previously done so in a tournament on Dutch television). Wade was also the first left-handed player to hit a live nine-darter.

DID YOU KNOW?

The first man to sell matched sets of brass darts was a Hungarian boiler linings salesman named Frank Lowy. He was the founder of Unicorn darts, still the largest darts manufacturer in the world.

DUTCH NINE

Raymond van Barneveld's fourth nine-darter was achieved on 29 April 2010 in Aberdeen against Terry Jenkins during the Premier League.

A TO Z OF PLAYER NICKNAMES

Tony Eccles   The Viper
Sue Edwards   Super Sue
Rilana Erades   Pebbles
Albertino Essers   Sensation
Alan Evans   The Welsh Wizard
Peter Evison   The Fen Tiger
Erwin Extercatte   Seabert

ON THE HOOF

Bullseye's most iconic and enduring personality is the cartoon character Bully. Few might have noticed though, that he was ambidextrous. In the opening credits of the show he was shown to throw his darts with his right hand (or hoof?), however prior to the show's ad break, he can be seen to write 'End of part one' using his left hand. Very smart for a bovine.

READ ALL ABOUT IT!

In the last competition before the Second World War, more or less the whole of England and Wales had been drawn into the News of the World Championship. The entry for the competition that year was between 250,000 and 260,000, and huge interest was generated by the London and South competition. In May it attracted a record crowd of 14,534 that filled the Royal Agricultural Hall in Westminster to witness the final. The unfancied Marmy Breckon took the title.

In 1939 an audience of more than 16,000 attended the London and South of England Regional Final at the Royal Agricultural Hall. An enormous electric scoreboard was used, the first of many technological features to be innovated over the years for the benefit of supporters.

During wartime the *News of the World* continued to support and give exposure to darts. It promoted its winners, organising charitable events, often supporting the Red Cross by way of their 'Team of Champions'. The core of the team were Jim Pike (captain), Leo Newstead, John Ross and Harry Head throughout the years of conflict. Other fine players were conscripted into the team when necessary. By the end of the conflict this group had raised £202,681 (in excess of £20 million in today's terms). As such, darts can truly be said to be a sport that more than most has helped win a war.

Via the NAAFI sports packs darts was a constant presence for Britain's service people serving at home and abroad, but it wasn't unusual for soldiers and sailors, particularly those made prisoners of war, to make their own ''arras' but maintaining the *News of the World* rules.

Darts had an important role in keeping up the morale of both civilians and service people overseas. Jim Pike was to argue that maybe the war was, in part, responsible for the development of the popularity of the game as it helped many people through the terrors of the conflict, offering a sense of comfort, a reminder of home, and some recreational activity.

As peace broke out, Allied service people and Axis prisoners of war from across the world, took darts, and the *News of the World* code, home with them, thus fostering the worldwide interest in the game.

News of the World Finals – 1938–39

Region/Winner	Club	Score
London & South		
Marmaduke Breckon	Jolly Sailor, Hanworth	2–1
Lancashire & Cheshire		
Peter Birchall	St Peter's Liberal Club, Oldham	2–1
Yorkshire		
Jim Munroe	Vine Tree, Wakefield	2–1
North		
Jimmy Young	Wheatsheaf Hotel, Newcastle	2–1
Midland Counties		
Harry Prior	Duke's Head, Polebrook	2–0

Region/Winner	Club	Score
Wales		
Charlie Parker	Castle Inn, Pontywaun	2–0

DID YOU KNOW?

The 2007 World Final was between Phil Taylor and Raymond van Barneveld. The game was tied at 6–6 in sets and van Barneveld had a 2–1 lead in legs. Barney then missed four darts and Taylor tied the set at 2–2. The set went to 5–5, and van Barneveld won the sudden-death leg to secure his fifth World Championship (four with BDO and one with PDC). Taylor had many opportunities to win the match, as he led 3–0, 4–2 and 5–3, and afterwards Taylor said, 'Of all the finals I've played in, I would probably put this one as the best.'

DUTCH NINE

Raymond van Barneveld's fifth nine-darter came in the 2010 World Matchplay on 17 July 17 2010 in his first-round match against Denis Ovens.

FOR THE RECORD

Dart players in Philadelphia, PA (the home of American-style darts) used to keep their dart points sticky by sticking them in potatoes.

VILLAIN

Ted Hankey is a two-time BDO World Professional Darts Champion and has built up a large following owing to his obsession with and resemblance to Dracula. His entrance is typically marked by him wearing a black cape and throwing rubber bats into the crowd, while he plays his darts with a trademark scowl.

Hankey, from that hotbed of darting talent – Stoke-on-Trent, took his first BDO World Championship title in 2000 and reached the final again in 2001, but lost to John Walton 6–2. He didn't reach another major final until his victory in the 2009 BDO World Championships.

In his first round match of the 2008 BDO World Championships, Hankey was drawn to meet Steve West. Twice Ted found himself behind in the match, recovering from 1–0 and 2–1 down to win the final two sets in succession. Afterwards, he attributed his erratic performance to a minority of the crowd who had jeered him throughout the match. He pushed on to the quarter finals where he was defeated 0–5 by Simon Whitlock. Again, he blamed sections of the crowd for his display, although during the match it had been Hankey who had received a warning from Barry Gilbey, the match referee, after he punched the board. Post-match, Hankey emotionally told the BBC's Ray Stubbs that he was thinking about quitting the sport, needing to consider his future.

The following day, in a BBC interview with Stubbs and Bobby George, Ted moderated his stance saying that he would take a break for a month, given that he was very disappointed with his performance against Whitlock and telling how he needed to work on the basics of his technique.

However, later on in the year, during the BDO International Open on 15 June 2008 in a quarter-final match with Robbie Green, Ted complained about the air-conditioning being turned off, something Green had requested, claiming his lighter darts were being caused to drift in mid-flight. In response Hankey threw his darts with deliberate lack of consideration, causing commentator David Croft to mark out his behaviour as 'disgraceful'. Hankey went on to lose the match 2–1.

During the 2009 BDO World Championship Hankey revealed his alcohol intake before commencing play was excessive and that generally he felt he was not taking himself seriously as a darts player. He began the 2009 Lakeside Championships with a first-round victory over close friend Brian Woods. The scoreline, of 3–0 in sets, was telling, as Woods had suggested before the match that Hankey would be 'lucky to get nil!' He then went on to win the Championship, overcoming Tony O'Shea 7–6 in the final.

During the 2009 Grand Slam of Darts Ted lost his opening group game 3–5 to Scott Waites, with the crowd once more on his back, calling out and booing while he was throwing, which visibly upset Ted. In a subsequent interview on ITV4 he told of his unhappiness with the situation, saying 'if that's the darts you want to play, then keep it.' He was subsequently fined £250 for his actions.

In the 2010 Grand Slam of Darts, despite getting an initial warm response from supporters (Hankey was smiling and taking on the pantomime villain role in good spirit) the crowd yet again got to him, booing as he threw his darts and ignoring requests from the referee to quieten down during the throws. Hankey was eliminated from the competition by Steve Beaton in the first knockout

quarter finals. He was taken to the final set in each of his first three rounds before losing to Wayne Mardle 5–4. At one point he was up 3–0 in sets.

WHAT THEY SAID

'At the end he effed and blinded at me. I'll see him upstairs in a minute and we'll see how big and brave he is.'

Phil Taylor on Chis Mason

'Is ballroom dancing a sport? It's recognised as a sport but I don't see any balls there.'

Bobby George

'I wasn't nervous during the match but the streaker certainly affected my game. I just wish I'd got her name and address!'

Shaun Greatbach following the Lakeside streaker's appearance in 2001

FOR THE RECORD

In June 1978, John Lowe achieved a 1,001 leg in 22 darts: 140-180-140-100-140-140-125 and ending on double 18. John averaged a fabulous 137 per throw and 45.6 per dart.

HERO

Stacy Bromberg burst into the top echelon of darts when she made the final of the 1995 Women's World Masters – the same year she won North American Open. Although she was beaten by England's Sharon Colclough in the Masters, seven years on, by then a Member of US World Masters Team and ranked the number one American woman, Stacy qualified for the BDO Women's World Darts Championship. She was once more defeated, this time by the Dutch former European (1998) and World Masters Champion (1999) Francis Hoenselaar (2–0). However, Bromberg had shown herself to be a formidable international campaigner.

In 1997 Stacy was chosen for the winning 'International' team that defeated Canada. However, 1999 was a watershed year on the world stage for her when she reached the semi-finals of the Australian Grand Masters, and gained selection for the US World Cup Team. This, alongside her double gold medal performance in the World Cup that same year (in the Women's doubles and the 'overall' category, in Australia) threw her into the limelight of global darts. By 2000 Bromberg had gained an impressive darts pedigree, being a five-time North American Open Champion, consistent membership of US World Masters Team and having gained victories in the Windy City Open (1997 and 1998).

Stacy's life today is filled with charity work. Donations have come from all over the USA, cheques for $5 or $1 bills have filled her post box and Stacy now has an annual Champions' Challenge which benefits the Make-A-Wish Foundation. In 2003, in her home town, Bromberg won the Women's Las Vegas Desert Classic, meeting the formidable Deta Hedman in the final, winning six of the ten legs played. Twelve months on Stacy found herself yet again in the final, but on that occasion was narrowly defeated (6–5) by the phenomenal Trina Gulliver playing at the top of her game.

In 2010 Stacy rolled aside the former world women's champion, Anastasia Dobromyslova (4–3) to make the first ever PDC Unicorn Women's World Championship final at Blackpool's Winter Gardens against Tricia Wright, who had claimed more than half a century of titles during her career. Wright held leads of 4–2 and 5–3 but failed to kill off the match. The pressure her opponent exerted caused her to miss four match-winners, leaving Bromberg to pocket the £10,000 title – then a record for the women's game.

Stacy has been battling cancer for the last 27 years and as a four-time cancer survivor, she dislikes dwelling on her battle with the disease, saying that 'everyone has their battles in life . . . I am no different.' For Stacy this personal struggle needs to remain personal, 'That's just how I deal with it,' she says. As such her stance is self-evidently noble and brave, distinguishing her sport and her as a quality human being.

In 2011 Stacy had been the US Women's number one player for 13 of the previous 16 years. At that point she had won the US Singles title for 12 consecutive years and was the Professional Darts Corporation Women's World Champion.

Bromberg is also involved with work with The Heart of Darts from its inception and recalls when the charity purchased its first wheelchair. She is the US Ambassador for the charity and takes this responsibility very seriously.

A TO Z OF PLAYER NICKNAMES

Bobby George	Mister Glitter or the King of Bling
Alan Glazier	The Ton Machine
Shaun Greatbatch	Nine Dart
Alan Green	Danger Scouse
Robbie Green	Kong
Tom Grevink	The Bono
Trina Gulliver	The Golden Girl

BULLY'S HOME

Up until its ninth series, *Bullseye* was recorded at ATV/ Central House in Broad Street, Birmingham. For the tenth series, it moved to Central's purpose-built studios at Lenton Lane in Nottingham, which became its home until 1995. The Challenge revival was made at Yorkshire Television's studios in Leeds, but for the *Gameshow Marathon* one-offs it moved to the London Studios on the South Bank of the Thames.

READ ALL ABOUT IT!

The first News of the World Championship after the Second World War was the competition's inaugural National Championship and the UK's first national darts competition (although while Wales and England were fully incorporated, Scotland was not). As can be seen from the finalists, it was truly of nationwide interest. It attracted an amazing 289,866 entrants.

The *News of the World* had previously backed away from developing a national contest because of the wide variation in 'house' rules and conditions throughout the UK. Such was the range of play that many accomplished darters turned their backs on News of the World competition for reasons such as unfamiliarity with the clock board used in the finals – a huge number of players had grown up with the London fives board and nothing else.

The 1948–49 final was held at Empire Pool, Wembley.

News of the World Finals

Year/Winner	Club	Score
1947–48 Harry Leadbetter	Windle L C, St Helens	2–1
1948–49 Jackie Boyce	New Southgate SC	2–1
1949–50 Dixie Newberry	Albert, Hitchin	2–0

DID YOU KNOW?

Historically, dartboards were fashioned out of elm wood. The numbers and wedges had to be painstakingly painted on and the wires (spider) took something like 100 staples to fasten to the board.

Apocryphally publicans sometimes just threw the board in slops and/or the spillage from their beer taps after closing time and hung them up to dry until the morning. This was said to be carried out in order to prevent boards from cracking. While it is more likely that beer (as a source of sustenance) might have been given to livestock (in particular pigs), boards would have needed to be regularly immersed in water, which also had the side effect of darts being less likely to fall out of ever-hardening wood. However, if carried too far, dousing would certainly have shortened the life of the board, and a good elm board could be quite a costly item.

In the early 1920s the Nodor company started to market clay boards in black and orange colours, supported by slogans like, 'The only perfect board' or 'Silent and everlasting'. However, this latter motto seemed to sum up the lack of popularity of the board. Although it did indeed last longer, it lacked the reassuring 'thunk' of a dart striking home that seemed to epitomise the game for most players. By the end of the decade Nodor was back to producing traditional elm boards.

The elm and cork targets were eventually replaced by boards made of tightly packed fibres of hemp or compressed East African, Brazilian or Chinese sisal, although cheaper boards are made of coiled paper.

Often normal levels of air moisture will tighten a board enough to keep it in decent trim. Overly dry conditions will see the board gradually degrade depending on the amount of use. This can to some extent be alleviated by exposing the board to steam (a boiling kettle or placing it over a bowl of hot water. I once knew a bloke who would occasionally take a board to the steam room with him – and was on a couple of occasions invited to diddle on the strength of it. Another chap insisted on taking his target to bed to keep it 'moist' (taking in the body moisture generated during the night), bringing a whole new meaning to 'bed and board'. Alternatively just wrapping a relatively dead board in a damp towel for a few hours can bring it back to life. However, if exposed to too much damp, sisal, hemp or paper boards will swell and bulge, the fibres falling out as a result, so creating what some folk call a 'fat board'.

WHAT THEY SAID

'The other day Phil was going on about how he could not get a set of tables and chairs in his Bentley. What does he want a Bentley for? It is pathetic, absolutely pathetic.'
Chris Mason on Phil Taylor

'Darts really can help with literacy.'
BBC presenter Ray Stubbs to Sports Minister Richard Caborn (Ray presumably meant numeracy)

'My wife says I'm not half the man I used to be, and she's not kidding.'
Andy Fordham after shedding 10 stone

FOR THE RECORD

In April 1987 Pat Irwin (playing in a double start/double finish 501 match), hit a staggering 170 in (bull-60-60) and a 170 out (60-60-bull) in the same leg.

A TO Z OF PLAYER NICKNAMES

Andy Hamilton	The Hammer
Ted Hankey	The Count
Paul Hanvidge	Polly Boy
Dennis Harbour	The Pearl
Rod Harrington	The Prince Of Style
Jamie Harvey	Bravedart
John Henderson	Hendo
Steve Hine	Muffin Man

WHAT THEY SAID

'Phil is lucky I'm not 10 years younger when my b******s were bigger than my brain. He is always giving it the "Bertie big"'.

Chris Mason on Phil Taylor during less friendly times

'It really is fit or bust now for Andy.'

Phil Taylor on the health of Andy Fordham

'You can't drink too many otherwise you can't see what you're throwing at.'

Eric Bristow

DID YOU KNOW?

At the 2008 UK Open, Phil Taylor broke the world record for the highest average in a televised game. He averaged 118.66 against Kevin Painter in the fourth round.

FOR THE RECORD

On 13 October 1984, in the quarter-finals of the MFI World Matchplay Championships between John Lowe and Keith Deller, Lowe hit the first televised nine-dart 501 game in the history of darts: 180-180-141 (treble 17, treble 18, double 18) claiming £102,000 for the feat. Due to tax implications, though, John was unable get his hands on the cash for two years.

HERO

Raymond van Barneveld is a five-times World Darts Champion, and two-times UK Open Champion. The argument that he is the most popular figure darts is all but confirmed by the chants of 'Barney Army' (which replicates the mantra of the most loyal of England cricket supporters, the 'Barmy Army'). Barneveld has a close relationship with his fans, shown regularly at the end of Premier League events when they chant 'Barney, give us a wave'. He never fails to respond with a smile. He has regularly praised the supporters of the Premier League.

From January to June 2008, Raymond was the PDC world number one ranked player. In total he has won 11 BDO Majors (4 World Championships, 2 World Masters, 3 World Darts Trophies and 2 International Darts league titles) as well as 4 PDC Premier Events (1 World Championship, 2 UK Opens, and 1 Las Vegas Desert Classic).

His victory in the 2007 PDC final, added to his four previous BDO Championships, brought him level with Eric Bristow as a five-times world champion, and he is one of only three players in darts history to achieve this. He is the most successful Dutch darts player of all time, and has a significant effect in putting the game of darts on the map in the Netherlands and continental Europe.

Barney's first World Championship appearance came in 1991, playing in the Embassy World Championship at the Lakeside Country Club, but his first round match ended in a 0–3 defeat to Australian Keith Sullivan. His first final was in the Finnish Open where he lost to Andy Fordham.

The 1995 World Championship saw Ray reach his first world final, but it ended in defeat 3–6 to Welshman Richie Burnett. The former postman took his first world title in 1998, beating Burnett in a repeat of the 1995 final. This match however is often listed among the greatest of all-time – having reached 5–5 in sets, van Barneveld finally took the title by winning the final set 4–2 in legs on double 8.

He successfully defended the trophy the following year by the same winning margin, this time against Ronnie Baxter. This made him only the third player in the tournament's history to have launched a successful defence of his title; the other two being Eric Bristow and Martin Adams.

His run of success ended in the first round in 2000, when Ray crashed out at the hands of Chris Mason, who averaged 100 and crushed van Barneveld's hopes of a hat-trick of titles.

He reached the final again in 2003 to clinch his third world title by beating Ritchie Davies 6–3. In 2005 he did not drop a set in the first three rounds as he beat Gary Anderson, Mike Veitch and Vincent van der Voort. A 5–3 semi-final win over Darryl Fitton and 6–2 triumph over Martin Adams in the final brought him that fourth title.

Barney reached his sixth final in 2006, and was aiming to equal Bristow's record of five BDO world titles, but his hopes were ended by lightning-quick 21-year-old compatriot Jelle Klaasen who prevailed 7–5.

He has also won the prestigious Winmau World Masters title on two occasions: once in 2001 when he recorded a win in the final over Jarkko Komula of Finland and again in 2005 when he beat Goran Klemme in the final. Other major tournament wins include the World Darts Trophy and the International Darts League.

In March 2006 Ray gave a 13–5 spanking to Colin Lloyd in the final of the International Darts League for his 11th BDO Grand Slam tournament. Moving away from the BDO, he won his first major PDC title in June 2006 by beating the Welshman Barrie Bates in the final of the UK Open at the Reebok Stadium, Bolton. Earlier in the day, he had knocked out Phil Taylor in the quarter-finals, accomplishing what had been a burning ambition. Ray beat Taylor again just weeks later in the semi-finals of the 2006 Las Vegas Desert Classic. He lost 6–3 to Canadian John Part in the final the following day.

Soon after this, van Barneveld began making alterations to his game: he changed his darts and began using the 'stacking' (or 'understacking') technique used by Taylor – this involves putting the first dart in the top of the 60 bed and stacking the next two underneath. The darts used were a gramme lighter than his old ones and cost the equivalent of £1 from a local store in Holland.

Taylor and van Barneveld met again in the 2007 PDC World Championship final, in a match which Taylor later described as the best final he had been involved in. From three sets down, Barney came back to beat Taylor 7–6 in the sudden-death leg in one of the greatest darts matches of all time. This matched Bristow's record of five world titles. In February of that year Raymond won the Masters of Darts tournament by beating Peter Manley 7–0 in the final with a 107 three-dart average.

Barneveld inflicted one of Taylor's heaviest defeats (11–4) in the quarter-final of the 2007 UK Open and went on to successfully defend his title, beating Vincent van der Voort in the final 16–8. In doing this, Barney became the first person to successfully defend the UK Open crown. A month later, he continued his haul of major titles by beating Andy Jenkins 13–6 in the final of the 2007 Las Vegas Desert Classic.

In addition to his four major titles (the World Championship, two UK Open Championships and the Las Vegas Desert Classic) Ray has added eleven non-televised PDC Pro Tour titles (five UK Open Regionals and six Players' Championships) to his personal roll of honour. In the 2009 Las Vegas Desert Classic he narrowly lost to Phil Taylor 13–11 in the final, but shortly after took another sabbatical from darts. There was speculation that he was considering retiring from the sport, however he stated after his first round win in the 2009 World Grand Prix over Alan Tabern that he was suffering from diabetes and that his absence was in order to get fit and healthy, putting in some gym time. He also attributed his relatively mediocre form at the time to the diabetes. Despite his problems in recent years, he still continues to be a major force to be reckoned with in the world of darts.

DID YOU KNOW?

Commentator John Gwynne's son, Andrew, is the Labour MP for Denton and Reddish.

FOR THE RECORD

On 18 December 1976, the Welshman Leighton Rees completed a game of 3,001 in 141 darts, counting on only the single and double bulls and finishing on a double bull. Rees hit no fewer than 34 double bulls and 52 bulls in this tremendous feat.

A TO Z OF PLAYER NICKNAMES

Andy Jenkins	Rocky
Terry Jenkins	The Bull
Ian Jones	The Whippet
Wayne Jones	Woody/The Wanderer

ISN'T THERE ANYONE ELSE?

Jim Bowen alleges that he was the fifth choice to host *Bullseye*. Apparently the first three turned it down flat and the fourth said he'd check his diary.

READ ALL ABOUT IT!

It was in the 1950s that Unicorn Products Ltd, started to manufacture duplicate darts, as used by particular News of the World Champions.

Tom Barrett, who had been entering the competition for years, reached the area finals on three occasions during the 1950s. He was to write that the event was 'the highlight of each darts season'. Both Tommy Gibbons (1951–52, 1957–58) and Tom Reddington (1954–55, 1959–60) won the title twice in the 1950s. No player was ever to claim the national title three times.

Between 1950 and 1958 the final was held at the Empress Hall, Earls Court, and throughout the decade and into the next, the Grand Finals attracted crowds of 12,000+.

The News of the World Finals

Year/Winner	Club	Score
1950–51 Harry Perryman	Home Office SC, Greenford	2–0
1951–52 Tommy Gibbons	Ivanhoe WMC, Conisbrough	2–0
1952–53 Jimmy Carr	Red Lion, Dipton	2–0
1953–54 Oliver James	Ex-Servicemen's Club, Onllwyn	2–0
1954–55 Tom Reddington	New Inn, Stonebroom	2–0
1955–56 Trevor Peachey	Black Fox, Thurston	2–0
1956–57 Alwyn Mullins	Traveller's Rest, Tickhill	2–0

Year/Winner	Club	Score
1957–58 Tommy Gibbons	Ivanhoe WMC, Conisbrough	2–0
1958–59 Albert Welsh	Horden Hotel, Seaham	2–1
1959–60 Tom Reddington	George Hotel, Alfreton	2–1

DID YOU KNOW?

When Ted Hankey whitewashed Ronnie Baxter 6–0 in the final of the 2000 BDO World Darts Championship, he won with in the most amazing way imaginable – with a 170 checkout. The final lasted a paltry 46 minutes and is the shortest in the Frimley-based competition's history to date. In the semi-final that year against Chris Mason, Ted Hankey scored a championship record 22 x 180s in a match. He also scored a record 48 x 180s over the course of the 2000 tournament.

REFEREE

Russ Bray is a PDC referee and is considered by many to be the best in the world at his craft. His calling career started after a regular caller failed to show up for a county match and he stepped in. Subsequently Russ was contracted to call for the PDC in 1996 and was given his debut at the World Matchplay in Blackpool. He was the caller when Phil Taylor hit the PDC's first-ever televised nine-darter in 2002 (Taylor was playing Chris Mason). He was again on call when Michael van Gerwen's achieved the same feat during the 2007 Masters of Darts in Hengelo. In June 2007 Russ was officiating over Taylor's nine-darter against Wes Newton and once more a year later when Taylor did it again against Jamie Harvey. Perhaps he's something of a good-luck charm?

Prior to the call to call, Bray was a county player for Hertfordshire and later played on the pro circuit, teaming up with Eric Bristow to win the Norway and Finland pairs. In addition to working in darts, he has made use of his distinctively raspy voice in commercial work over recent years. He was the referee in the PDC's first ever video game, *PDC World Championship Darts*, and also undertakes commercial voiceover work.

A TO Z OF PLAYER NICKNAMES

Mervyn King	The King
Jelle Klaasen	The (Young) Matador
Jarkko Komula	Smiley

MORE THAN BFH

The first two *Bullseye* programmes were so flawed that they were scrapped and never broadcast. This was especially expensive because a car had been won in one of them.

DID YOU KNOW?

The most popularly used dartboard, and the one used at all big events, is what we know as the 'London board' (because it was initially most popular in London). However, this target is among around half-a-dozen broadly similar boards in common use. The arrangement of the numbers on the London board is often attributed to Brian Gamlin, a carpenter from Bury, Lancashire. Apocryphally Gamlin came up with this composition in 1896 when he was 44. However, many argue that it was in 1913 that Thomas William Buckle gifted the world with its most-used dartboard. This was affirmed by his son, Thomas Edward Buckle, in 1992. He also suggested that Gamlin might have come up with the Manchester board (see below).

The East End board is divided up into twelve sections or 'pies' (the London board has 20 segments of course). Clockwise, from the top, the sections are numbered 10, 20, 5, 15, 10, 20, 5, 15, 10, 20, 5, 15. The East End board has ¼ inch (or sometimes slimmer) double and treble rings.

The Yorkshire or Doubles board is similar to the London board but lacks an outer bull. It has no triple ring and a slender ¼-inch doubles ring (the London board has ³/₈ inch rings). Occasionally you come across these boards with totally black faces.

The Staffordshire or Burton board more or less mirrors the Yorkshire board; however it has two diamond-shaped scoring beds outside the doubles ring. One is set between the wire numbers 14 and 9 on one side; the other is between the 4 and 13 on the opposite side. These segments each have a value of 25 points, and are sometimes used as an out shot on that number. The Staffordshire board also has an outer bull.

The Tonbridge board is not unlike the Yorkshire board, however, where the latter has doubles these appear as trebles on the Tonbridge board and doubles are scored on triangular beds on the inside of these trebles.

The Manchester board, sometimes known as the 'Log-End' board, has a number arrangement of (clockwise from the top) 4, 20, 1, 16, 6, 17, 8, 12, 9, 14, 5, 19, 2, 15, 3, 18, 7, 11, 10, 13. This board is not as big as others, having just a 10-inch playing diameter, with ¼-inch doubles.

All these boards continue to be used to some degree, with variations across regions. There are several other types of board but many have been lost in the mists of time.

WHAT THEY SAID

'I don't read books.'

> Eric Bristow (let's hope he makes an exception
> in this case . . .)

'Before a match I like to relax with 25 bottles of Holsten Pils and six steak and kidney pies.'

> Andy Fordham on his MySpace page before he was
> taken seriously ill in January 2007

'It's in his genes – it's in his 501s. Cushty-wushty.'

> Bobby George commentating on Andy Fordham

REFEREE

Martin Fitzmaurice is a darts master of ceremonies extraordinaire – a caller, scorer and referee who has been involved with the BDO since 1985, for many becoming the face and voice of the Embassy World Championship and all the other major tournaments which are organised under the BDO/WDF banners.

Martin, who made his tournament debut at the 1975 Buckham Oil Open, introduces the players after delivering his well-known catchphrase, 'Are you ready? Ladies and Gentlemen . . . LET'S . . . PLAY . . . DARTS!'

Fitzmaurice was born in Kensington in 1940 and has held a variety of jobs in his eventful life, ranging from working in a solicitor's office and as an electrician to being a tube train driver.

Fitzmaurice's first foray into the world of darts came in 1975, when he and his family had moved to Essex. At a pub in Colchester, he was asked to keep the scores in a local match, and that was the beginning of a long career.

After refereeing a youth match (also in Essex), darts legend Bobby George asked Martin if he would referee for him in exhibition matches when his regular referee Freddie Williams was unavailable. Fitzmaurice accepted and he and the King of Bling worked together for about 5 years.

It was at the World Masters in 1985 that regular caller Jack Price was taken ill, and consequently Bobby George nagged the BDO to use his referee. Thus Martin was given the role and made it his own. A chalker at the 1986 Embassy World Final, the first time the tournament had been held at the Lakeside Country Club at Frimley, Martin was later the caller/referee.

On 9 January 1990, when Paul Lim became the first player to achieve a perfect nine-dart finish in the World Championships against John McKenna, Martin Fitzmaurice was the referee.

He now acts as Master of Ceremonies at BDO tournaments. Besides his career as a referee and MC, he is also very active within the BDO and the International Dart Players' Association (IDPA).

FOR THE RECORD

Vic Cutts and Pete Hotchkins, playing at the Eagle in Nechells, Birmingham, totalled 460,740 points to set a 24-hour two-man record in September 1989.

The highest score in 24 hours by a lone man is 567,145 hit by Kenny Fellowes at the Prince of Wales, Cashes Green, Stroud, on 28–9 September 1996.

A TO Z OF PLAYER NICKNAMES

Mark Landers	Sparky
Cliff Lazarenko	Big Cliff
Adrian Lewis	Jackpot
Paul Lim	The Singapore Slinger
Al Lippman	Iceman
Colin Lloyd	Jaws
John Lowe	Old Stoneface/The Legend

READ ALL ABOUT IT!

Tom Barrett became the first player to retain the national championship (1963–64, 1964–65 – while sponsored by Unicorn). In 1961 and 1963 he got to the London finals and in 1962 he made the Grand Finals. Barrett was on hat-trick the following year but a handful of matches short of the final he was stopped by former Welsh Champion Bill Harding, in a 2–0 defeat at Battersea Town Hall in the London and Home Counties Divisional Final.

The Empire Pool, Wembley, played host to the finals between 1959 and 1962. In 1963 it was held at Alexandra Palace (where it remained until 1977).

Following Barry Twomlow's victory in 1969 he joined Unicorn, becoming the firm's darts ambassador and played a major part in widening of the popularity of the game across the world. Many fine darters, like John Ross, argued that Twomlow was 'one of the greatest dart players who have ever lived'.

News of the World Finals

Year/Winner	Club	Score
1960–61 Alec Adamson	Prince of Wales, Hetton-le-Hole	2–1
1961–62 Eddie Brown	Magpie, Stonham	2–0
1962–63 Robbie Rumney	Waterloo Hotel, Darlington	2–0

Year/Winner	Club	Score
1963–64 Tom Barrett	Odco SC, London	2–0
1964–65 Tom Barrett	Odco SC, London	2–1
1965–66 Wilf Ellis	Brookside WMC, Upton	2–1
1966–67 Wally Seaton	Swan, Parson Drove	2–0
1967–68 Bill Duddy	Rose & Thistle, Frimley Green	2–0
1968–69 Barry Twomlow	Red Lion, Chesterfield	2–0
1969–70 Henry Barney	Pointers Inn, Newchurch, Isle of Wight	2–0

FOR THE RECORD

Gravel-voiced referee Russ Bray hit the bullseye on a standard dartboard from 10ft away, outdoors, on Blackpool's North Pier, and in doing so, achieved a Guinness world record. Russ improved on the previous best of the day, 9ft 6in, which was set by Scott Gibling, Bray's fellow PDC colleague.

YOU DEFINITELY CAN'T BEAT A BIT OF BULLY!

By the end of its original run, *Bullseye* was receiving 12,000 applications a year to appear on the show and there was a 5-year waiting list just to be in the audience!

WHAT THEY SAID

'I think of myself as an athlete because I have been on *Grandstand* and I wear trainers.'

Andy Fordham

'I feel like I want my mummy.'

Bobby George at the prospect of live TV work without any script or autocue

'I'm flying to China and Japan – if you think Beckham is a big name, you should see me there.'

Phil Taylor

THE MAN BEHIND THE MIKE

John Gwynne is a Sky Sports commentator for PDC darts tournaments as well as being a reporter on *Soccer Saturday*. Prior to joining Sky to cover darts, Gwynne was regularly heard on BBC Radio Lancashire, covering Lancashire County Cricket. BBC Radio Manchester employed him for over a decade to cover Oldham Athletic matches.

Away from the lip-mike, Gwynne is an after-dinner speaker and writes for a darts magazine.

FOR THE RECORD

In July 1989, during an exhibition at the Bell, Cox Heath, Maidstone, Alan Glazier literally dazzled the crowd with his brilliance. He claimed victory in each of the 13 matches he played, and topped-off the performance with a 21-dart 1,001 leg (and in doing so missed out on the world record by just three darts). His scores were: 140-135-124-140-180-120-161. His 161 out shot was achieved by hitting a treble 20, treble 17 and bull.

A TO Z OF PLAYER NICKNAMES

John MacGowan	Mr Magoo
Kevin McDine	Supa Mc
Steve Maish	Mr Magic
Crissy Manley	Two Dart
Peter Manley	One Dart
Wayne Mardle	Hawaii 501
Chris Mason	Mace The Ace
Gary Mawson	The Mauler
Colin Monk	The Mad Monk

BULLY'S BIOG

A celebrity Christmas special of *Bullseye* in 1986 included Fatima Whitbread making the most of the somewhat tangential connection between javelin throwing and darts.

WHAT THEY SAID

'Nah, I don't watch TV . . . apart from a few sports programmes. I just don't have the time.'

Eric Bristow

'I used to be called "the whippet".'

Andy Fordham

'Painter didn't play well early on – you could say he was up and down like a paint brush.'

Bobby George (turning to some DIY commentary)

'I have been to Buckingham Palace and 10 Downing Street but cannot get on the BBC. I am very disappointed because it boils down to snobbery.'

Phil Taylor quoted long before he gained recognition in the BBC Sports Personality of the Year poll

'It wasn't a fluent performance from me but I tried my heart out.'

Mark Dudridge, on losing the 2005 world final to Taylor

FOR THE RECORD

In November 1989, during the qualifying for the Winmau World Masters, county player Martin Golder, representing Norfolk, threw a very respectable 39.12 one-dart average in four legs. He threw two 14-darters, a 12-darter and topped it off with an 11-dart game where he hit 41-180-180-100.

A TO Z OF PLAYER NICKNAMES

Dale Newton	The Artful Dodger
Wes Newton	The Warrior
Paul Nicholson	The Asset
Phil Nixon	Nixy/The Ferry Hill Flyer
Alan Norris	Chuck

DID YOU KNOW?

In the PDC World Championship final of 2009, Phil Taylor's 110.94 three-dart average was the highest ever recorded in a World final. His average over the course of the entire tournament was an astounding 104.08.

CAN'T GET ENOUGH OF BULLY

Bullseye is regularly repeated on satellite channels, including Challenge. Let's hope they continue to do so. The show still has a cult following to this day, and it is the subject of a 'Bring Back Bullseye' campaign which is active on Twitter and Facebook.

DID YOU KNOW?

Flights fashioned from authentic turkey feathers are becoming more difficult to get your hands on as smaller turkeys are now popular and they produce unsatisfactory feathers.

WHAT THEY SAID

'I've got a nice little crafty deal with the people in Barbados; 10 days out there teaching the locals how to play darts for an hour a day. Get paid for that as well.'
Eric Bristow

'I hope for his sake he has a long and illustrious career. But when he finds out what women are all about we'll see, won't we?'
Martin Adams on the young Michael van Gerwen

FOR THE RECORD

In Manchester during a charity event in 1989 Tony Jones recorded 28 perfect 180s in just 1 hour and 25 minutes.

A TO Z OF PLAYER NICKNAMES

Colin Osborne   The Wizard
Tony O'Shea   Silverback
Denis Ovens   The Heat

A VILLAIN ON THE OCHE

In 1989, John Cooper, who was later identified as a serial killer, appeared on *Bullseye*. He would later be convicted of multiple burglaries, armed robberies, and in 2011, following advances in forensic science, two double murders, one rape and a sexual assault. Footage of his appearance on the show was later used by the prosecution to match him to witness reports at the time.

READ ALL ABOUT IT!

The News of the World Championship became the first nationally televised darts tournament when ITV broadcast the 1970 event. With the exception of the 1986 competition, which failed to be broadcast because of a strike by technicians, ITV covered the event for the remainder of its existence. During this period the competition could attract up to 8 million viewers.

This decade saw the darts 'boom' – a time when players became household names. Sponsorship and prize money was generous, and players had really never had it so good. In 1974 the 34-year-old Leighton Rees was strongly fancied to take the title but he never got into his stride and he lost to the US's Al Lippman 0–2 in the preliminary round. Two-time, back-to-back United States Champion, and the first American to be taken seriously on the world darts stage, Al Lippman was one of America's first generation of darting stars in the British tradition, the majority of whom hailed from the Philadelphia area. Known for keeping calm and balanced under fire, on his day he could match any player in the world and is among the best male darters to come out of America. Al passed away on 23 November 1976, but he lives on as a legend of the game in the USA. Consistent and modestly dignified, Lippman was a naturally gifted player. He owned a corner bar in the Fishtown district of Philadelphia. Short, double-chinned, usually offering a kind smile, he was generally to be found with his shirt collar open and sleeves rolled up, revealing intricate tattoos. Although a ferocious competitor, he had endless patience and was always ready to teach and advise.

Bobby George became the only player to win the tournament without losing a leg in 1978–79, while Swede Stefan Lord (1977–78, 1979–80) became the fourth player to win the title twice and the first and last non-British player to become champion.

News of the World Finals

Year/Winner	Club	Score
1970–71 Dennis Filkins	Barrow, Hepburn & Gale SC, Bermondsey	2–0
1971–72 Brian Netherton	Welcome Home Inn, Par	2–0
1972–73 Ivor Hodgkinson	Great Northern, Langley Mill	2–1
1973–74 Peter Chapman	Bird in Hand, Henley	2–1
1974–75 Derek White	Belvedere Inn, Weymouth	2–1
1975–76 Bill Lennard	Cotton Tree Inn, Manchester	2–0

Year/Winner	Club	Score
1976–77 Mick Norris	King of Denmark, Ramsgate	2–0
1977–78 Stefan Lord	Stockholm Super Darts Club	2–0
1978–79 Bobby George	King George V, Ilford	2–0
1979–80 Stefan Lord	Stockholm Super Darts Club	2–0

The 1960s and '70s saw the popularity of darts in Ireland grow swiftly and in 1973 the News of the World Championship arrived in the Emerald Isle with the prize of a place in the 1974 Grand Finals at Alexandra Palace. The Republic was divided into eight areas with the respective winners being brought together in Ballsbridge, Dublin, to play in the first Divisional Finals at the Royal Dublin Society.

News of the World Championship
Eire Division (1970s)

Year	Champion
1974	Jim McQuillan
1975	Jack McKenna
1976	Shay O'Brien
1977	Shay O'Brien
1978	Jim McQuillan
1979	Eddie Morrissey

DID YOU KNOW?

Peter Manley became a tennis tipster for 180bets.com after announcing that he had been a Surrey junior tennis champion.

FOR THE RECORD

Between 26/7 August 1988 at the Eight Bells in Ewell, Paul Finch, Graham Prior and Nick Steggell scored 2,093 double bulls and 7,861 single bulls. I'll bet they needed a pint after that – which was handy . . .

A TO Z OF PLAYER NICKNAMES

Kevin Painter	The Artist
John Part	Darth Maple
Dennis Priestley	The Menace

LOOK AT WHAT YOU COULD HAVE WON

Speedboats as star prizes seemed to be a feature of *Bullseye*. It was even rumoured that the producers had done a deal with a speedboat manufacturer. Co-host Tony Green once commented ironically to a losing pair: 'Never mind, boys, look at what you could have won – see, it was a speedboat . . . that would have come in handy in Wolverhampton, wouldn't it?'

DID YOU KNOW?

At 8.15 p.m., on Thursday 28 May 1936, the BBC Regional Service, for the first time, broadcast darts from The Horns pub in Kennington; the finals of 'The Team Championship of London'. Thereafter darts continued to turn up now and again on the BBC regional network. On 25 November 1937 a match from the Hanbury Arms, featuring that hostelry's team and a side from the Caledonian Arms, Islington, constituted the first broadcast of a local derby. On 9 March, 1938 the West of England Championship darts was broadcast for the first time on West of England radio.

WHAT THEY SAID

'His darts used to stick out like tulips in the board.'
Bobby George on Vincent van der Voort

'I'm certainly getting more people recognising me since winning the world title.'

Martin Adams

A TO Z OF PLAYER NICKNAMES

Mario Robbe	The Dutch Robot
Gary Robson	Robbo/Big Robbo
Alex Roy	Ace of Hearts

WHAT THEY SAID

'Sex is an anti-climax after that.'
**Alan Warriner-Little reflects on his victory over
Roland Scholten to gain a place in the 2003
PDC World Championship semi-final**

'I won't be able to stop the drinking just like that but
I've hopefully cut it in half and if you cut what I drink in
half that is a hell of a lot.'
Andy Fordham

CHARITY BEGINS AT THE OCHE

Bullseye included a charitable element that took place
at the start of the second half of the show. It involved a
professional darts player or other celebrity throwing nine
darts and the score they achieved would be converted
to cash to be donated to the charity of the final pair's
choice. Any score over 301 was doubled. At the end of
series 5 onwards, the player with the highest score in the
series received the coveted Bronze Bully trophy.

In previous years celebrity players received a start of
60, but later, the charity challenge was solely taken on by
professional dart players. Celebrity players hardly ever
perfomed above a mediocre level. George Best missed
the board completely (but looked like he might have
been partaking of the liquid delights of the green room
beforehand). Unimpressive perfomances with the darts
by celebrities were often bolstered by the individuals
offering to add some of their own money to the charity
pot.

DID YOU KNOW?

On 19 April 1938 the first broadcast of a ladies' darts was featured on the regional network of the BBC. It came from the Adam and Eve pub in Homerton, London, and covered the Ladies' Individual Darts Championship.

WADDELLESE!

Super Sid Waddell is the undisputed voice of darts. He is a mad Northumbrian elf-like wordsmith whose descriptions of dart-related events feel akin to some kind of surreal poetry from another world (Planet Alnwick maybe?) interpreted via a velvet meat grinder. He strings words together that should make no sense at all, but given proper time for interpretation, they fall into shape. Drawing sentences and metaphors from a plateau somewhere between Punk pernod and Baudrillard's back yard, Sid is an allegory within his own Simulacra and Simulation.

Here are a few of Sid's outbursts which defy belief (there'll be more scattered throughout the book):

'That's quality with a capital K!'

'That was like throwing three pickled onions into a thimble!'

'They'll be welcoming Jocky Wilson back to Kirkcaldy as if he was the Ayatollah Khomeini!'

SID YOU KNOW?

Sid Waddell read Modern History at Cambridge University. Aside from his work in darts, he has written several books and the hit 1980s kids' TV show *Jossy's Giants*.

FOR THE RECORD

Darts-mad Allen Chaperlin and Ian Melton played 1,265 games of 501 in 182 hours and 1 minute at the Eagle Tavern, Oxford. That equates to a game every 8.6 minutes and in all the feat took more than 7½ days to achieve.

A TO Z OF PLAYER NICKNAMES

Lionel Sams	The Lion
Josephus Schenk	The Orange Machine
Roland Scholten	The Tripod
Tomas Seyler	Shorty
Ronnie Sharp	Pancho
Kirk Shepherd	The Karate Kid
Andy Smith	The Pieman
Dennis Smith	Smiffy
John Snijers	The Black Beauty
Brian Sørensen	Brice
Graeme Stoddart	Toon Shark
Co Stompé	The Matchstick
Mensur Suljovic	The Gentle

WHO HAS THE HONOUR?

The highest *Bullseye* charity score was achieved by the Welshman Alan Evans who hit 401 during the 1984/85 series. His efforts of 180, 180 and 41 with nine darts were impressive. However, there is an ongoing debate about this as Evans' last treble 20 fell out of the board, though it had clearly hit the treble 20. So, purists argue that Eric Bristow holds the record score for the nine charity darts with 380, along with Mike Gregory who matched that score subsequently.

READ ALL ABOUT IT!

Darts became a regular television feature all through the 1970s and early '80s, but interest declined and by 1988 events like the British Open, the Professional Championship and Gold Cup as well as World Cup team tournament all vanished from the nation's screens.

Jocky Wilson, the then current Embassy Champion, was well fancied to take the News of the World title in 1982. The previous year's winner, Bobby George, and Alan Evans also qualified, however a total outsider from Shropshire, Roy Morgan, walked away as the winner.

Eric Bristow became the fifth player to claim a News of the World double (1982–83 and 1983–84) and only the second player to retain the championship. Later in the decade Bobby George made himself a two-time title holder (1978–79, 1985–86) as did Somerset's Mike Gregory (1986–87, 1987–88). Mike, the seventh and final double winner, was also the last person to retain the title.

Jocky Wilson was back in the Grand Finals in 1989 at the Hammersmith Odeon but was again thwarted. He was beaten by the eventual champion Dave Whitcombe in the second round.

Steve Beaton and Peter Evison were the bookies' choice in 1990 but it was Peter Cook from Wiltshire who captured the first prize of £8,000. The last final of the 1990s (1989–90) took place at the Docklands Arena, London. Paul Cook emulated Bobby's George's feat of not losing a leg on the way to winning that last title of the decade, and was presented with an engraved set of darts to commemorate his achievement.

The News of the World Finals

Year/Winner	Club	Score
1980–81 John Lowe	Willow Tree, Pilsley	2–0
1981–82 Roy Morgan	Wheel o' Worfield, Worfield	2–1
1982–83 Eric Bristow	Foaming Quart, Norton Green	2–0
1983–84 Eric Bristow	Milton Hayes BC, Stoke-on-Trent	2–0
1984–85 Dave Lee	Ivor Arms, Pontllanfraith	2–0
1985–86 Bobby George	Old Maypole, Hainault	2–0

Year/Winner	Club	Score
1986–87 Mike Gregory	Stones Cross Hotel, Midsomer Norton	2–0
1987–88 Mike Gregory	Stones Cross Hotel, Midsomer Norton	2–1
1988–89 Dave Whitcombe	King's Head, Ipswich	2–1
1989–90 Paul Cook	Gorse Hill WMC, Swindon	2–0

WADDELLESE!

'That could be a total eclipse of the Part.'

'Painter's not bothering with an undercoat . . . He's gone straight to gloss!'

'Painter, back arched like a toreador.'

REFEREE

John McDonald took over from Phil Jones as Master of Ceremonies on his retirement from the PDC. Living in London, he has worked for the organisation since February 2007. Previously John was a boxing announcer for Barry Hearn. He has experience in various world championships such as boxing, snooker, pool, bowling and fishing. McDonald made his debut in darts during the 2004 confrontation between Andy Fordham and Phil Taylor, and following that, he officiated at the 2005 World Matchplay and the 2006 Premier League.

DID YOU KNOW?

Peter and Chrissy Manley's daughter Sarah was a member of the indie band The Long Blondes.

FOR THE RECORD

Between 28/9 March 1986 an amazing darting extravaganza took place: four chaps – Graham Innis, Graham Miller, Graham Parker and Richie Davis – scored 1,003,769 in 24 hours at the Maxilla Club in London. They banged home 152 180s.

The highest darts score in one hour by a men's team is 21,944. This was achieved by Molson Coors North East All Stars at Marske Cricket Club in Cleveland on 9 September 2009.

A TO Z OF PLAYER NICKNAMES

Alan Tabern	Tabby/The Saint
Bob Taylor	The Bear
Phil Taylor	The Power
Mark Thompson	The Fire/The Fire Starter
Robert Thornton	The Thorn

DID YOU KNOW?

The first broadcast of an international match was made on Friday 5 May 1939. It featured a team from Torquay playing against a side from Londonderry, which the West Country outfit won by 3–2. The following month, Ben Travers, the famous playwright and broadcaster, alongside writer and broadcaster A.G. Street, commentated on a 'live' game between their respective pub teams.

WADDELLESE!

'Phil Taylor's got the consistency of a planet . . . and he's in a darts orbit!'

'Steve Beaton, he's not A-donis, he's THE donis.'

'If you had to throw a knife at your wife in the circus, you'd want to throw it like that.'

FOR THE RECORD

In 1989 Richard Smith of Carlisle completed a 25-dart 1,001 leg. He racked up 140-100-100-95-180-140-100-122-24.

BULLY'S BIOG

In early series of *Bullseye*, Jim Bowen usually mentioned the ITV region from whence the contestants hailed, except if they came from Northern Ireland when it was always 'over the water'.

A TO Z OF PLAYER NICKNAMES

Raymond van Barneveld	Barney
Jan van der Rassel	The Project
Michael van Gerwen	Mighty Mike
Vincent van der Voort	Greased Lightning

ARE YOU ASKING ME OR TELLING ME?

Believe it or not, one contestant on the Dave Spikey version of *Bullseye* appeared to believe that every country had its own sun.

DID YOU KNOW?

On 11 October 1939 the BBC Home Service broadcast a team darts match between Air Raid Wardens and Firemen. Thirteen days later another game featuring the Balloon Barrage Squadron of the RAF and an anti-aircraft battery of the Royal Artillery was covered. A week before Christmas a 'challenge match' pitting the City of London Police War Reserves against the London County Council Auxiliary Ambulance Drivers concluded this trilogy of 'service-based' darts coverage.

WADDELLESE!

'Steve Beaton, the Adonis of darts – what poise, what elegance – a true Roman gladiator with plenty of hair wax.'

'Eat your heart out Harold Pinter; we've got drama with a capital D in Essex.'

'There's no one quicker than these two tungsten tossers.'

FOR THE RECORD

In a charity throw at the 1988 British Professional Championships, a team made up of Bob Anderson, Eric Bristow, John Lowe, Chris Johns, Martin Phillips, Alan Warriner, and Ritchie Gardner established a 15-minute fast-scoring record of 8,806 points.

FOR THE RECORD

The highest score achieved by a team of eight women is 830,737 by the ladies of the Cornwall Inn, Killurin, Wexford, within a 24 hours between 1 and 2 August 1997.

A TO Z OF PLAYER NICKNAMES

James Wade	The Machine
Robert Wagner	The Magician
Scott Waites	Scotty '2' Hotty
Les Wallace	McDanger
Mark Walsh	Walshie
John Walton	Boy
Alan Warriner-Little	The Iceman
Darren Webster	The Sniper
Mark Webster	Webby
Tony West	The Tornado/Triple T
Robbie Widdows	Black Widdow
Jocky Wilson	Jocky/The Wee Scot
Paul Wilson	Mr Wils
Simon Whitlock	The Wizard of Oz
Dean Winstanley	Over the top
Brian Woods	Pecker
Ken Woods	The Executioner
Peter Wright	Snake Bite
Tricia Wright	The Wright Stuff
Darin Young	Big Daddy
Talisa Zwart	Smiley

READ ALL ABOUT IT!

The continuing demise of darts as a spectator sport saw the suspension of the News of the World Championship in the 1990s. However, Sky Sports and the *News of the World* revived the contest in 1996.

Phil Taylor was later to recall that Eric Bristow, his long-time mentor, had teased him for having failed to win the tournament, but his victory in June 1997, winning him the News of the World 'Big D' Trophy, £42,000 in prize money and a solid gold set of Unicorn darts, made up for all the jibes, and as he said at the time, 'I've won five world titles, but this one means everything.' Taylor had beaten Martin Adams, the England captain at the time, 2–1 in the last four of the competition.

After the event was wound up, only the World Professional Championships endured as a televised competition. A number of leading players, denied the opportunity to make the most of their talents, became frustrated with the way their game was organised, and within two years they had formed their own organisation.

But the public response to the oldest mass participation darts competition was less than hoped for and the *News of the World* decided to bring it to a conclusion.

News of the World Final

Year/Winner	Club	Score
1996–97		
Phil Taylor	Cricketers Arms, Newcastle-under-Lyme	2–0

BEST OF BULLY

The *Bullseye* tune was voted the best game show theme in a 2008 survey for Churchill Insurance.

DID YOU KNOW?

At 9.25 p.m. on Saturday 29 May 1937, London Television (BBC) broadcast the first televised darts coverage from Alexandra Palace. The programme, *Darts and shove ha'penny*, included a match between 'two well known hostelries'.

The BBC went for it again on 5 February 1938 featuring a confrontation between the *News of the World* champions and a quartet making up a BBC team. 30 April saw yet another darts broadcast bringing a BBC foursome up against a Press Club quartet. On 13 January 1939 a return match was covered.

The first 'local derby' was televised by the BBC on 15 October 1938. Teams of four from Islington and Lambeth battled it out in front of the cameras.

WADDELLESE!

'There's only one word for that – magic darts!'

'Even Hypotenuse would have trouble working out these angles.'

FOR THE RECORD

On 19 June 1987 at the Fishing Boat Inn, Northumberland, Tab Hunter scored a 23-dart 1,001 leg. He did it by picking off the following: 100-180-140-125-140-100-140-76. He averaged a creditable 43.5 points per dart, ending the final 76 in two.

CELEBRITY DARTERS' NICKNAMES

Sam Allardyce	The Dudley Destroyer
Steve Backley	Steveo/Long Throw
Vicki Butler-Henderson	The Vixen
Keith Chegwin	Cheggers
James Hewitt	The Galloping Major
Michael Le Vell	Spirit
Rowland Rivron	Right Here
Neil Ruddock	Razor
Phil Tufnell	The Cat
David Ulliott	Devilfish
Johnny Vegas	The Saint
Holly Willoughby	Hard to Beat

MR DARTS

Oliver Croft set up and ran the BDO from its inception in 1973. After a lifetime's tireless work administrating the sport of darts, he was awarded the OBE in the Queen's 2004 Birthday honours.

DID YOU KNOW?

Phil Taylor supports his home town football club, Port Vale and his one-time protegé Adrian Lewis is a rival Stoke City fan.

FOR THE RECORD

In June 1987 at the Now Inn in Crumlin, Gwent, Tony Elleson scored a perfect double start/double finish 301 game. While this might not sound unusual in itself, after his first throw he broke a shaft retrieving his darts and literally had to sit down for five minutes and dig out the remains before finishing his game. Certainly the stoppage of play did not affect his concentration: double 20-60-60-60-57-double 12.

THANK YOU FOR THE MUSIC

No one knows why, how, where or exactly when it started, but walk-on music, echoing the world of boxing, has come to be part of the darts universe. Now, although (as you can see) some players chop and change their musical introductions, fans, hearing just the first few bars of a star's theme, will know who is being called to do battle. Perhaps, like the warriors of the ring, darters choose their music to stir a passion or drive deep within their soul; something of the spirit that will make that crucial scintilla of difference between them and their foe. It might summon courage, put out a warning to evoke fear in an opponent or just bring a smile, a memory or an idea at a point of massive tension. Whatever the motivation or inspiration, listed below is a selection of what sends some of the world's greatest players on their marches to victory or defeat, joy or despondency, continued fame and fortune or the shadows of their game's history. Watch out for more later in the book.

'A Kind of Magic' – Queen	Steve Coote
'Ace of Spades' – Motorhead	Chris Mason
'Bad' – Michael Jackson	Steve Farmer
'The Bartender and the Thief' – Stereophonics	Mark Webster
'Be On Your Way' – DJ Zany	Ted Hankey
'Big Bad John' – Jimmy Dean	John Henderson
'Bonkers' – Dizzee Rascal	Steve Hine
'Boom Boom Boom' – The Outhere Brothers	Steve Farmer
'Breathe' – The Prodigy	Steve Maish Michael van Gerwen
'Bullet in the Gun' – Planet Perfecto	Stephen Bunting
'Burning Love' – Elvis Presley	Steve Maish
'Burn In My Light' – Mercy Drive	Alex Roy

THAT'S WHAT I CALL A DARTS FAN

I met Rakesh Navaratnam, from Selangor in Malaysia, at the 1980 BDO World Championships in Stoke-on-Trent. He had made the 6,500-mile trip to Jollees Cabaret Club to support his darting hero Bobby George. Not so bad if you make the 13-hour non-stop flight, but Rakesh started his journey with a 1,600-mile jaunt through Thailand, Burma and Bangladesh into India astride a 1960 Lambretta LI150. Unfortunately his ancient mechanical steed gave up the ghost in Kolkata, but undeterred he travelled on by bus, train and by hitching, making his way across India, Pakistan, Afghanistan, Iran and Turkey. He got himself a sturdy second-hand bike (a 'Triumph Traffic Master') in Izmir and cycled the 1,300 miles or so to Ostend in Belgium where he crossed the Channel. He got to Jollees after a 10-week journey just four days before George met Dave Whitcombe in the second round. Incidentally, Bobby was beaten in the final by Cliff Lazarenko, but Rakesh left for home with Bobby's autographed photo. Whether he made it back or not is another thing because as we left Jollees he found his bike had been nicked.

DID YOU KNOW?

James Wade dated *Soccer AM* presenter Helen Chamberlain but the pair split after about a year together. The couple had reportedly 'drifted apart'. Wade admitted it hit him hard, even affecting his darts.

REFEREE

George Noble made his first steps on stage after the regular county caller called in sick. George's talent was obvious from the start and after just two years he was making the then biggest darts stage in the world, Lakeside, his own. He officiated in every BDO World final at Lakeside from 1995 to 2007. Noble started his exhibition work with Bobby George and since then he has worked with all the great names, past and present. George is regarded by many as the best tournament referee on the planet and he very rarely makes a mistake on stage. Noble was the referee during the first Barneveld v Taylor match in Holland, at the Masters of Darts.

It took Noble until 2 January 2009 to cover his first nine-dart leg. It was at the Alexandra Palace when Raymond van Barneveld completed the feat against fellow countryman Jelle Klaasen in their World Darts Championship quarter-final match.

FOR THE RECORD

At the 1990 Embassy World Championships, Paul Lim of San Bernadino, California, threw a perfect nine-dart 501 leg. Because he did it in front of the TV cameras he received £52,000 for his remarkable achievement.

THE MYSTERIES OF DARTITIS

Dartitis is a very real nervous condition that can affect players at any time. It can have a serious impact on players' performance and seems to appear without warning.

Players suffering from dartitis seem to be struggling with a psychological problem that impairs their technique and often delays their release of the dart at the right moment. A famous case of this occurred in Richie Burnett, who was reported to have experienced the condition in 2009. The former World Champion was clearly suffering while playing in the first round of the UK Open, where he ended up losing in the first round to Alex Roy. Two years earlier Mark Walsh had fallen out of the top 32 as a result this malady, but by 2008 he was recovering and a year later he won four PDC Pro Tour events.

Eric Bristow said of his experience of the condition, 'It took me about 10 years to get rid of. I'm all right now, though . . . I'm throwing some nice darts at the moment, but every now and then I get a bit of a jump. I wish I could find a cure, I'd make a bloody fortune!'

If further proof were needed about the reality of this condition, the word dartitis was accepted, after much gathering of evidence, into the *Oxford English Dictionary*.

DID YOU KNOW?

When the National Darts Association (NDA) was formed in 1924 there were only eight leagues in existence. In February 1937 the *Daily Herald* claimed that there were more than 3,000 darts clubs and over 100 darts leagues in Britain. Within a year there were nearly 200 leagues affiliated to the NDA alone, with more than a quarter of a million players registered with the association. 'Unofficial' players were estimated to make the game of interest to millions.

WALKING ON

'U Can't Touch This' – MC Hammer	Andy Hamilton
'Chelsea Daggers' – The Fratellis	Roland Scholten Scott Waites
'Club Foot' – Kasabian	Paul Nicholson
'Cold as Ice' – Foreigner	Alan Warriner-Little
'Cotton Eye Joe' – Rednex	John Walton
'Crazy Nights' – Kiss	Eric Bristow Wes Newton

PDC events broadcast on Sky feature 'Chase the Sun' by Planet Funk before every ad break. This is the tune the crowd join in with their 'Oi-oi-ois' to. Very catchy.

FOR THE RECORD

Cliff Lazarenko threw his first nine-dart 501 at an exhibition at the Aberlynon Leisure Centre. Using 25-gram titanium tungsten darts, he hit two 180s and a treble 20, treble 19, double 12 for the 141 out in the last match of the evening.

DID YOU KNOW?

There was a *Bullseye* before *Bullseye*. A serious darts contest broadcast on BBC2 for two series in 1980 and 1981 was broadcast under the same title. The ITV programme began less than three weeks after the BBC show ended.

DOING THE MATH

After starting a school darts club Philip New, Year 6 head at Woodland Middle School, in Flitwick, Bedfordshire, noticed an appreciable change in the attitude of club members to maths, while at the same time their ability in the subject seemed to take a leap forward.

Subsequently Philip developed a programme that starts with a breakdown of the dartboard and which is followed by fast questioning to improve and develop the mental calculation skills of the pupils. From this point an interactive white board, projecting a giant dartboard, is used by the children to calculate scores and share how they go about making calculations.

New developed a range of other activities based on collecting and recording data and adapted the dartboard to create bespoke lessons, focused on the objectives and ability of groups of children and available time. This brought benefits not only in maths, but also in English, while giving the children a good opportunity to work independently on particular projects as part cooperative groups and teams.

To the delight of the kids Bobby George supported the programme by coming into the school to show how he, and other top dart players, use and hone their mental arithmetic skills.

For New, using darts has given a novel and useful feature to his teaching of maths and he is thrilled that the children can see learning maths as fun; something that can be enjoyable. Darts – the great educator!

WALKING ON

'Daddy Cool' – Boney M	Darin Young
'Don't Stop me Now' – Queen	Ronnie Baxter
	Phil Nixon
	Brian Woods
'Don't Worry be Happy' – Bobby McFerrin	Gary Robson
'Dynamite' – Taio Cruz	Dennis Smith
'Eat it' – Weird Al Jankovic	Andy Smith
'Enter Sandman' – Metallica	Wayne Jones
	Niels de Ruiter
'Ecuador' – Sash	Davy Richardson
'Eye of the Tiger' – Survivor	Peter Evison
	Raymond van Barneveld

WADDELLESE!

'Eat your heart out Isaac Newton, that was an apple falling!'

'He's like a hippo in a power shower.'

'Well as giraffes say, you don't get no leaves unless you stick your neck out.'

FOR THE RECORD

In the British Dart Organisation (BDO) Sikh players are exempt from the rule forbidding headgear.

GREAT, SUPER, SMASHING

Bullseye host Jim Bowen allegedly took to saying 'smashing' as a sort of reflex. After one contestant told Jim he was unemployed, he responded with 'Smashing'.

LONGEST? NOT THE LONGEST?

In May 2011 the Holland Sentinel carried a report on Ryne Du Shane and Dylan Smith, who made an attempt on the world record for the longest game of darts with a marathon session that started on a Monday morning and stretched into early hours of the following Wednesday at the Itty Bitty Bar in Park Township, West Michigan, USA.

Close to the 30-hour mark on the Tuesday afternoon, the two 19-year-old college students were tired but on schedule to break the Guinness world record of 35 hours and 25 minutes by 5.30 p.m. At that point their legs were sore from walking backwards and forwards to the board, and their attention was starting to waver.

They wrapped medical tape around their fingertips to prevent their skin from rubbing raw on the darts and the pair kept going until 2.00 a.m. on the Wednesday morning, in order to extend their lead on the existing record.

At the time of writing the pair needed to collect witness statements and file the paperwork required by Guinness World Records. Their total time in front of the dartboard was 41 hours.

Until that point the longest singles darts marathon was 26 hours and 42 minutes and was achieved by Stephen Wilson and Robert Henderson at the Glenisle inn, Palnackie, Dumfries and Galloway on 20/21 June 2008.

DID YOU KNOW?

At an exhibition match at Crystal Palace in July 1977, Muhammad Ali faced former Welsh champ Alan Evans. With Evans scoring only on triples, Ali won hitting a bullseye on the way out and immediately proclaimed himself darts champion of the world.

WADDELLESE!

'Look at him as he takes his stance, like he has been sculptured, whereas Bobby George is like the Hunchback of Notre Dame.'

'He's about as predictable as a wasp on speed.'

DID YOU KNOW?

The average speed of a dart hitting a board is around 64kph (40mph).

WALKING ON

'Fanfare for the Common Man' – Aaron Copland	Phil Taylor
'Flash Gordon' – Queen	Mark Dudbridge
'Fog On The Tyne' – Lindisfarne	Kevin McDine

BULLSEYE CATCHPHRASES – THE BOWEN YEARS

'Keep out of the black and in the red, there's nothing in this game for two in a bed.'

'Look at what you could have won.' (Yes, it's a speedboat, and you live in a top-floor flat, so never mind)

'And Bully's Special Priiiiize!' (The holy grail of the prize board, and more often than not, a Betamax video recorder)

'You win nothing but your BFH . . . your Bus Fare Home.' (A warning about what could happen if you lose the gamble)

'I've got £140 here and it'll take me two minutes to count it out.' (Jim's stock phrase going into a commercial break)

'The subjects that are lit are the ones you can hit.'

'You've got the time it takes for the board to revolve.' (Not long to decide to gamble or not, especially with the baying studio crowd all contradicting each other)

'Listen to Tony.' (Who will tell you to take your time . . . and you won't)

'Let's check that with Bully.' (For the spelling question in round one, Jim would check the contestant's answer with Bully, who'd walk across the bottom of the screen leafing through a dictionary)

DARTING LEGIONNAIRE

It was 1972 and I had just arrived in Marseille. I was planning to make my way along the A50 to the Foreign Legion selection centre in Aubagne, which was either the worst or the best idea I'd ever have – I still haven't decided. Wandering round looking for somewhere to eat I found a pretty grotty bar close to the *Cité Radieuse* (Radiant City) area, or as the locals call it *La Maison du Fada* (The House of the Mad). I asked the waiter the best route to Aubagne for a hitcher. It turned out that he was a former legionnaire who had served during the Algerian war, but as a young man he, Mathieu, who came originally from Lille, had worked in London, so in the empty bar our conversation blossomed. On finding out my penchant for darts my new friend invited me to play Javelot.

The game, some call it 'French Darts', is played mostly in the north of France and makes use of darts that are more like spears. These weapons, that can weigh anything from 250g to 400g, are fashioned from wood with steel tips and their flights are made out of a bunch of turkey feathers. You throw them underarm, 20ft or so, at a target whose scoring area is a small bull.

We played in a semi-covered area at the back of the bar and several games and more than several cognacs later, I got it! By now the locals were drifting in and I spent the rest of the day playing for drinks and eating seemingly endless servings of croutes. I probably won more than I lost because I didn't get to Aubagne the following day as planned, spending most of it unconscious in a hammock kindly slung-up by Mathieu in a tiny upstairs room above the bar. I had truly ate, drank and slept Javelot.

DID YOU KNOW?

Adrian Lewis's got his nickname (Jackpot) following a visit to a casino while competing at the 2005 Las Vegas Desert Classic. He 'won' a massive $75,000 jackpot on the slots, however, he was unable to claim the money as he was under age according to United States gaming laws. Gutted. Good job he made up for it by pocketing a hefty wedge for winning the 2011 PDC World Championships with a 7–5 victory over Gary Anderson.

WADDELLESE!

'When Alexander of Macedonia was 33 he cried salt tears because there were no more worlds to conquer – Bristow is only 27.'

'Like the lion in winter, like the leopard in the snows of Kilimanjaro, Lowe is full of experience; he will survive.'

WALKING ON

'Give It Up' –   Vincent van der Voort
  KC and the Sunshine Band

Darts crowds have now caught on to this one with their own rendition – 'Na-na-na-na-na-na-na-na-nananaaaa, Vincent van der Voort, van der Voort, Vincent van der Voort!'

BULLSEYE CATCHPHRASES – ON DAVE SPIKEY'S WATCH

'You've had a good night out, but you go home wi' nowt!'

'Throwers and knowers.' (How Spikey referred to the dart players and question-answerers)

'They risked it, they missed it!' (For losing gamblers)

DID YOU KNOW?

Phil Taylor holds records for high-scoring in darts. His three-dart average per match records are the highest in the history of the game.

WADDELLESE!

'He's playing out of his pie crust.'

'Darts players are probably a lot fitter than most footballers in overall body strength.'

FOR THE RECORD!

The most solo 180s hit in 24 hours is 123. The record was achieved by Duncan Swift at the Felixstowe Dock Sports and Social Club.

WALKING ON

'Hawaii Five-O' – The Ventures
'Hell Raiser' – The Sweet
'Hey Baby' – DJ Ötzi
'Hey ya' – Outkast
'House of Fun' – Madness
'Hungry Like The Wolf' – Duran Duran

Wayne Mardle
Dennis Priestley
Tony O'Shea
Roland Scholten
Barrie Bates
Martin Adams

DID YOU KNOW?

Bullseye's co-presenter, scorer and referee Tony Green was born in Belgium. He was a former county player (for Lancashire) before becoming the BBC's commentator for the World Professional Darts Championship.

In December 2010, it was announced on the BDO website that Green had been diagnosed with cancer and that he would not be well enough to commentate on the 2011 Lakeside World Darts Championship. Tony had previously worked on the commentary team for the tournament every year since it began in 1978.

DID YOU KNOW?

Eric Bristow became the first darts player to receive an MBE. He did so on 21 February 1989 at Buckingham Palace. Bristow admitted he was nervous about meeting Her Majesty the Queen, saying, 'It was more nerve-racking than any TV final.'

NINE-DART TAYLOR

The first time Phil Taylor achieved a televised nine-dart finish was at the Winter Gardens in Blackpool, against Chris Mason in the World Matchplay Championship in 2002. He has achieved the feat eight further times on television, including four times in the UK Open at the Reebok Stadium, Bolton (in 2004, 2005, 2007 and 2008).

On 24 May 2010, in the final of the 2010 PDC Whyte & Mackay Premier League, Taylor became the first player in professional darts to hit two nine-dart finishes in a single match.

The Power's nine-darters

Date	Opponent	Tournament
1/8/2002	Chris Mason	World Matchplay
5/6/2004	Matt Chapman	UK Open
12/6/2005	Roland Scholten	UK Open
8/5/2007	Raymond van Barneveld	International Darts League
9/6/2007	Wes Newton	UK Open
7/6/2008	Jamie Harvey	UK Open
15/9/2009	John Part	Championship League Darts
24/5/2010	James Wade	Premier League Darts
24/5/2010	James Wade	Premier League Darts

Among the prizes Phil has bagged for the feats listed above are cash (ranging from £50 to tens of thousands), an Opel car and enough Budweiser lager to fill a swimming pool (almost).

WALKING ON

'I got a feeling' – Black Eyed Peas	James Wade
'I'm gonna be (500 miles)' – The Proclaimers	John Henderson Robert Thornton
'Infinity 2008' – Guru Josh	Gary Robson
'I Predict a Riot' – Kaiser Chiefs	Dave Chisnall Kevin Painter
'Is this the way to Amarillo?' – Tony Christie	Peter Manley

DID YOU KNOW?

Peter Manley got his nickname after becoming known for hitting doubles with his first dart . . . hence 'One Dart'.

WADDELLESE!

'That's like giving Dracula the keys to the blood bank.'

'That's the greatest comeback since Lazarus.'

'He's stringing them together like a blind fisherman mending a net.'

'I don't know what he's had for breakfast but Taylor knocked the Snap, Crackle and Pop outta Bristow.'

IT'S A FUNNY OL' GAME!

Two nuns walk into a pub. They went up to the bar and ordered a couple of pints and after asking for the darts one strolled up to the oche and threw a single twenty. Her second dart thudded home in the treble twenty. She looked around the bar and to see that she had acquired something of an audience. Turning her focus back to the board, she rolled her not inconsiderable shoulders and let the last arrow fly with such gusto that that Steve Backley would have been proud of it. However, as she let go, her companion, readying herself for her turn, took the dart right between the eyes. To the horror of everyone present she collapsed to the floor.

As the crowd gathered round the stricken sister, a woman pushed her way through the throng, yelling, 'Look out! I'm a nurse'. Swiftly, the pack of onlookers parted, allowing the angel of mercy access to the injured party. After a minute or so of examination, the latter-day Nightingale stood up and after a considered pause shouted, 'One nun dead and eightyyyyyyyyyyyyyyyy!'

FOR THE RECORD!

The record for 'around the board on doubles' by a solo man, at a throwing distance of 9ft and retrieving his own darts, is 2 minutes 13 seconds. This was achieved by Bill Duddy (News of the World Champion 1967–68, finalist 1974–75) at The Plough, Haringey, on 29 October 1972.

WALKING ON

'Jump Around' – House of Pain   Gary Anderson
'Jungle Rock' – Hank Mizell   Lionel Sams

TAYLOR ON THE TELLY

Phil Taylor's achievements in darts have led to guest appearances on television. In 2009, he cameoed in *Coronation Street*, playing the part of 'Disco Dave', the captain of a rival darts team to the Rovers Return. In 2011 he was seen handing over the award for Best Comedy Panel Show at the British Comedy Awards. Also in 2011 he finally appeared on an edition of *A Question of Sport*.

DID YOU KNOW?

No player has a winning head-to-head record against Phil Taylor. He has a 79 per cent win rate against Raymond van Barneveld, the player with the most wins against him.

NO NEED TO ANSWER

Jim Bowen once asked a contestant, 'In which state of the USA was President Kennedy assassinated in Texas?'

WADDELLESE!

'By the time of the final on Sunday he should be fit to burst!'

Sid on Jocky Wilson

'Keith Deller's not just an underdog, he's an under puppy!'

DARTS GLOSSARY

Arrows	A slang term for darts
Bag O' Nuts	Scoring 45 points in a throw
Barn Dart	When the third dart of a throw hits the target you were aiming at for with the first two darts
Barrel	The part of the dart where you grip it
Bed	A section of a number
Bombs	Very large or heavy darts
Bones	When you need to hit a double 1 to win
Bull	The centre of the board, the area is divided into two sections (the single & double bull)
Bull Out	Winning the game with a double bull
Bull Up	Throwing at the bull to decide which player will throw first
Busting	Scoring too many points when trying to finish a game

FOR THE RECORD!

The 'Million and One' record for a team of eight was achieved at the Weigh Inn Bar in Omagh, Northern Ireland, and took 35,698 darts, averaging 84.03. In the process the team hit 1,342 140s and 371 180s. The marathon lasted close to 46½ hrs.

WALKING ON

'King Kong' – Big T Tyler   Robbie Green
'King of Kings' – Motorhead   Steve Farmer
'Kung Fu Fighting' – Carl Douglas   Co Stompé
                                                        Kirk Shepherd

ROYAL RUMINATIONS

Eight days before Christmas 1937, King George VI and his other half, the Queen Mother to be, then Queen Elizabeth, were visiting a community centre in Slough. Her Majesty asked some dart players if she might have a go; she scored a single 7, a 13 and a single 1. This was followed by three darts from the hand of the king after which he declared that he had been beaten by 2 points.

In 2007 Zara Phillips met Phil Taylor at the BBC Sports Personality of the Year event, and told him that her grandmother (Her Majesty the Queen) loved watching the game on television. Taylor told how Zara also revealed that the Queen Mother was also a fan, so she clearly never lost the bug.

AWAY GAME

It was 1978 when along with a few friends, I thought of making my way to the Heart of the Midlands Club in Nottingham, to take in the BDO World Darts Championships. We set out on a fresh but fine morning in early February, waiting for the transport promised by Fat 'Arry. 'Arry, weighing in at about 8 stone and close 6ft tall, drove up in a Reliant Robin that looked like it had not only seen better days, but also that its days were numbered; it coughed like consumptive chain saw.

'Jump in' cried 'Arry to the five of us staring at the pathetic heap as it shuddered in the gutter.

As you can imagine, the journey to Nottingham was a challenge. Three of us crushed into the back seat, two in the front passenger seat, swapping turns at sitting on one another's laps. However, early doors our trails were not helped after 'Arry decided to show off what he called an 'hoptional hextra'. It seemed he had loaned the vehicle from his old school chum, 'Lefty' Dex, vice-secretary (or something) of the local Communist Party. It had been deployed in canvassing during 1974 General Election, helping to pull in the few dozen or so votes for a workers' paradise in Newham, and still had it public address system installed (complete with megaphone on the roof). With a flick of a switch, as we pottered towards the M1, the Soviet Red Army Choir smashed out the 'Internationale', provoking more than a few odd expressions from passers-by and one or two straightforward insults.

Looking politely impressed at first, after about 10 minutes there was a general request to 'give it a rest'. 'Arry obligingly flicked the switch back to its original position, but the sound of the committed comrades trundled on regardless. We took it in turns to hit the dashboard, and leaning out of the window we even tried giving the megaphone a thump, but nothing worked; they just kept on belting it out. Heightening the sense of the macabre, the music seemed to slow down and speed up in sympathy with our transport. Hence, when we got up to our top speed on the motorway, which must have been all of 35mph, the comrades were banging it out like the Chipmunks.

Amazingly we got to the club unmolested. We had come with the specific motivation to support Londoners Alan Glazier and Eric Bristow, who both got knocked out in the first round, Bristow not really getting off the ground with a 6–3 defeat by American Conrad Daniels and Glazier beaten by Welshman Alan Evans 6–4. With John Lowe being the only Englishman left in the competition we decided to make our way home.

However, 'Arry had made a new friend, Beryl. She was a big girl among big girls, and she had always wanted to go to London, so 'Arry turned into the travel fairy to see to it that her wish was granted. How we all got into the Reliant remains a mystery to this day. I spent half the journey with my face buried in parts of Beryl. She never ceased to be amused by her propensity to, what she called, 'bottom burp', screaming with laughter, saying 'oh, s'cuse me duck', each time she laid out a foreboding and noxious gas cloud in what had become the Black Hole of Calcutta on three wheels. It seemed to take us days to get back to the East End. We dawdled southward with our socialist accompaniment all the way.

Oh yes – John Lowe got the final only to be beat the Leighton Rees (11–7) making the 38-year-old from Ynysybwl (which translated means 'Island in the Pool' for anyone who wants/needs to know) the first World Darts Champion.

DID YOU KNOW?

Phil Taylor is the first player to win more than £1 million in prize money.

DARTS GLOSSARY

Chalk(ing)	Keeping score
A 'Classic'	Scoring 26 points in a round by hitting a single 5, single 20 and a single 1
Cork	The bullseye
Cracked	Hitting a single when aiming at a double

WALKING ON

'Land Down Under' – Men at Work	Tony David Simon Whitlock
'Life is Live' – Opus	Mensur Suljovic
'Loch Lomond' – Runrig	Jamie Harvey
'London Calling' – Clash	Eric Bristow
'Lust for Life' – Iggy Pop	Jamie Caven
'Monster' – The Automatic	Colin Lloyd

ROYAL RUMINATIONS

On a Sunday evening in January 2009 another of the Queen's grandchildren and eleventh in line to the throne at the time, Peter Phillips (brother of Zara), turned up at the BDO World Darts Championship in Frimley Green, Surrey. Sporting an Elvis-style wig and a cowboy hat, young Peter drank lager and cheered on the players with gusto. On spotting the royal among the crowd, BBC commentator David Croft declared: 'I've seen the lot now. Royalty, in an Elvis wig . . . in a cowboy hat. Your grandma would be so pleased. He's a top lad. Loves his darts.' In all Peter spent eight hours watching the darts, accompanied by a large group of revellers which included the England rugby player Mike Tindall.

LET'S HAVE A JOLLY OLD GAME OF DARTS

In 1937 variety artist and songwriter Leslie Sarony composed 'The Dart Song' commissioned by the *News of the World*. He recorded this ditty with the Leslie Holmes and the Jack Hylton Orchestra in London as the 'Two Leslies'. It was subsequently released on 23 April, on His Master's Voice records. A snip at 6d, it was marketed as 'The 'News of the World' signature tune for the Individual Darts Championships' and 'Specially Composed by The Two Leslies'. The same year the song was also recorded by Billy Cotton and his Band on Rex Records. It went on for 2 minutes and 45 seconds

DID YOU KNOW?

In the final of the Taylor Walker Ladies' Championship, on 21 May 1937, at the Ironbridge Tavern, East India Dock Road, London, the finalists, Mrs Gotobed (of the Bishop

Bonner) and Miss Ring (the Duchess of Kent, Islington) played two games, both demonstrating 'amazing skill'. Miss Ring, who was just sixteen, won both games.

WADDELLESE!

'As they say at the DHSS, we're getting the full benefit here!'

'There hasn't been this much excitement since the Romans fed the Christians to the Lions!'

'The players are under so much duress, it's like duressic park out there!'

WOMEN!

While women are still quite some way from gaining equality in darts, their participation in the sport has been a constant throughout its history. During the first 'golden era' of the game as a mass participation sport, in the late 1930s the *Darts and Sports Weekly News* provided regular reports on ladies' matches, including some notable results against men. Following the frequent questioning about women's involvement in darts, in October the editor declared that 'No mere man will stop them.'

The Brewers Journal of April 1938 announced that it was 'happy to note that in this darts boom women were taking their part.' It had been breweries that had initiated knockout tournaments for women, played out in pubs, at the same time they argued that the presence of women would lead to better conditions in the hostelries they served. Remember this was a time not long after prohibition of alcohol in the USA, something that was pushed for in the UK many times over the first few decades of the twentieth century.

DARTS GLOSSARY

Dead	hitting the exact score required
Diddle for the Middle	throwing at the bullseye to see which player will throw first
Dirty Darts	derogatory slang for questionable tactics
Double Bull	the centre portion of the bullseye
Downstairs	the lower portion of the dartboard
Double In	hitting a double to start a game
Double Out	hitting a double to win a game

ROYAL RUMINATIONS

In January 2011 Prince Harry was downing pints at Alexandra Palace watching the World Darts Championship, in particular Gary Anderson and Adrian Lewis, who both won their semi-finals. The prince had made his entrance unnoticed while the lights were down, and he sat in the VIP area with a number of friends, including former England rugby star, Will Greenwood.

However the fans cheered after he was spotted on the big TV screens among the 2,500 audience. Commentator Sid Waddell told how he had, 'seen Harry at Twickers for the rugby, but I never thought I'd see the day when he turned up at Ally Pally for the darts!'

Harry, seemingly having a great time, yelled and cheered along with the crowd, waving his '180' sign with the best of them. On winning, Lewis told how the prince jumped out of his VIP seat to congratulate him, 'Prince Harry came up to me after the match and gave me a hug. You don't expect that when you come from Stoke.'

SHEER POETRY

The 'Laureate of Darts' Noel E. Williamson immortalised many great players and the game in general with his musings. Typical of his classic lines was this stanza from 'Thank you Eric', a tribute to Eric Bristow:

> And Bristow has the M.B.E.,
> A credit to his name,
> And to all who helped to organise
> Our favourite indoor game!

DID YOU KNOW?

Phil Taylor won the 2006 PDC Player of the Year award at the inaugural PDC Awards Dinner on 9 January 2007. It was held at the rather plush Dorchester Hotel in Park Lane, London.

WADDELLESE!

'His face is sagging with tension.'

'The fans now, with their eyes pierced on the dartboard.'

'He's been burning the midnight oil at both ends.'
Sid's insight into Keith Deller's nocturnal habits

DARTS GLOSSARY

Fallout   slang for scoring with a dart when you
            intended to hit another number
Fat   the largest portion of a number (the area
            between the double and triple ring)
Flight   the 'feathers' of the dart

FOR THE RECORD!

The most bulls (individual) record is 1,320. This record
is held by John Lowe at the Unicorn Tavern, Chesterfield,
Derbyshire, on 27 October 1994.

WALKING ON

'One Step Beyond' – Madness   Darryl Fitton
'Paranoid' – Black Sabbath   Colin Osborne

DARTS ANIMALS

There isn't much of a history of the involvement of animals in darts. Some older aficionados of the game might recall the apocryphal 'Pipey', a Jack Russell type mutt of dubious heritage, whose master was the notorious East End criminal and First World War hero, Isaac 'Darky' Bogard. Every time Bogard scored a bullseye Pipey would stand on his back legs and perform a back-flip at which point it was customary for everyone witnessing the feat to provide the dog with his 'nobbins' – throwing loose change into Pipey's hat (a tattered bowler placed in front of the dog by Darky). Failure to contribute would mean incurring Bogard's displeasure, a man not indisposed to attacking people with an 8lb lump hammer. As such, most folk seemed generously appreciative of Pipey's antics.

DARTS GLOSSARY

Game On	a call for silence at the start of the game
Game Shot	the winning shot
Good Group	a compliment for tight, accurate throwing (all three darts in the triple for instance)
Hat-trick	scoring all three darts of a turn in the bull
High Ton	scoring between 151 and 180 points in a game

FOR THE RECORD!

The highest score, retrieving own darts (achieved as a doubles team), is 465,919. This was achieved by Jon Archer and Neil Rankin on 17 November 1990 at the Royal Oak in Cossington, Leicestershire.

WADDELLESE!

'Under that heart of stone beat muscles of pure flint.'
Sid on Old Stoneface himself – John Lowe

'The pendulum swinging back and forth like a metronome.'

WALKING ON

'Rabbit' – Chas & Dave
'Reach Up' – Perfecto Allstarz
'Rhinestone Cowboy' –
  Glen Campbell

Eric Bristow
Adrian Lewis
Bob Anderson

DID YOU KNOW?

Phil Taylor was voted the 2007 Fans' Player of the Year following a poll conducted on the website Planet Darts.

DARTS ANIMALS

'The Winker' is another renowned creature of the oche. A one-eyed, semi-retired racing pigeon, he became the lucky mascot of a darts team playing out of the Connaught public house in North Woolwich, London, when the twentieth century was young. In a run of over 150 matches the team only lost a dozen or so games, but their feathery talisman was never present on the occasion of a defeat. Endearingly, for a homing pigeon, most of his absences were because his owner, Reg Revins (a well-known football scout locally and darts poet) got lost en route to away fixtures. Sadly 'The Winker' was eventually to meet an untimely end, getting himself run over by a pony and trap while taking a breather near Wrotham in Kent toward the end of a race. A new amulet, Rolf, a plump, aging hamster, following a handful of fairly unsuccessful outings, went missing during a home game. It was eventually concluded that he had been designated supper by the Connaught's cellar cat, Captain Bridges; sport being not so much a dog-eat-dog as a cat-eat-hamster affair in this event. The Connaught team, not able to face the future 'Winkerless', disbanded.

WADDELLESE!

'He looks about as happy as a penguin in a microwave.'

'He's as slick as minestrone soup.'

'Jocky Wilson, he comes from the valleys and he's chuffing like a choo-choo train!'

'It's the nearest thing to public execution this side of Saudi Arabia.'

'His physiognomy is that of a weeping Madonna.'

'He's as cool as a prized marrow!'

DARTS GLOSSARY

Leg	a game in a match, as 'the best of five legs', in which each leg is an entire game
Low Ton	scoring between 100 and 150 points in a game
Madhouse	double 1 to win a game
Mugs Away	slang term for rule that allows the loser of the previous game to start the next game immediately (without diddling for the middle)
Oche	the throwing line

FOR THE RECORD!

The record for the most doubles scored in 10 hours is 3,266 (from 8,451 darts). This was achieved by Paul Taylor at the Lord Brooke, Walthamstow, on 5 September 1987.

WALKING ON

'Satisfaction' – Rolling Stones	Steve Duke Snr
'Sex on Fire' – Kings of Leon	Jelle Klaasen
'Sharp Dressed Man' – ZZ Top	Rod Harrington
'Song 2' – Blur	Tony West
'Special Brew' – Bad Manners	Mark Walsh
'Stayin' Alive' – The Bee Gees	Steve Beaton
'Superman' – Infinity	Matt Clark

DARTS ANIMALS

Perhaps the most noteworthy of darting beasts was 'Judas', an orang utan who sailed the seven seas on a succession of insalubrious merchant vessels in the 1930s. Judas, or as he was known in some South American ports, 'El Muno de la Flecha', was accompanied to dockside taverns and touted, given a 50 start, to better the score of any taker with ten darts. Bets were laid on primate or human, usually Judas being offered at anything from 3-1 upwards. Fuelled by copious amounts of rough rum, the happy ape was successful enough to have changed hands several times, either by purchase of theft. However, Judas was always going to come to a sticky end. It was in Bintulu, during a match with Carlo, a proboscis monkey, that things turned nasty. Judas was shot to death just about as he was about to throw his tenth and winning arrow (if it had managed to hit the board) – Carlo had scored 31 in nine darts, Judas had a total of 30, when it got all too much for a bloke who had put his shore pay on the monkey. El Muno de la Flecha was buried in the South China Sea, a nautical and sporting legend.

DID YOU KNOW?

Phil Taylor was made an inaugural inductee to the Stoke-on-Trent Sporting Hall of Fame on 7 January 2010, after his fifteenth world championship victory.

DARTS GLOSSARY

Pie	any of the numbered sections on the dartboard
Robin Hood	when one dart sticks into the back of another
Round	any three dart turn
Round of 9	throwing three triples in one turn
Route 66	scoring 66 points in a round

FOR THE RECORD!

The 10-hour record for the most trebles is 3,056 (from 7992 darts). This was achieved by Paul Taylor at the Woodhouse Tavern in Leytonstone on 19 October 1985.

TAYLOR v BARNEY

As Phil Taylor was taking all before him in the PDC, Raymond van Barneveld was the dominant force with the BDO. However, this separation of the best in darts denied fans the chance of seeing two of finest players on the planet compete against each other on a regular basis. However, van Barneveld came over to the PDC in 2006 and met with Taylor in the Premier League Darts tournament. This contest concluded in a 7–7 draw. The return match went in Taylor's favour. Barneveld's first PDC victory over Taylor came that same year in UK Open. The 11–10 quarter-final success was followed by a 4–3 semi-final victory for the Dutchman in the Las Vegas Desert Classic. Taylor later defeated van Barneveld 3–1 in the World Grand Prix.

The next big tournament that brought these two giants of the game together was the 2007 PDC World Championship at the Circus Tavern. The final has been described as the greatest game of darts ever played. Despite being 3–0 up at one point, Taylor was defeated by Barney 7–6 in a sudden-death leg in the thirteenth set. Taylor responded to this loss by defeating van Barneveld on two occasions in the 2007 Premier League Darts and beating him in the final of the inaugural US Open, although van Barneveld later defeated Taylor 11–4 in the quarter-finals of the UK Open. Taylor lost his top spot in the PDC World Rankings to Barney in January 2008, but regained it the following June.

In major PDC tournaments in 2008, Taylor twice claimed victory over van Barneveld in the Premier League, lost by 10–9 in the quarter-finals of the UK Open, but won the World Grand Prix against his adversary 6–2. The rivalry continued into 2009 with the two meeting in the World Championship final for a second time; Taylor won 7–1. The two then met in the 2010 World Matchplay final where Taylor won 18–12.

At the time of writing, Phil and Ray have met more than 45 times, with Taylor claiming the lion's share with 35 victories.

WALKING ON

'The Heat is On' – Glenn Frey	Dennis Ovens
'The Imperial March' (Darth Vader's Theme, *Star Wars*)	John Part
'The Saints are Coming' – The Skids	Alan Tabern
'Tom Hark' – The Piranhas	Jamie Caven
'Town Called Malice' – The Jam	Shaun Greatbatch

DID YOU KNOW?

Phil Taylor's right forearm is insured for an astounding £20 million.

WADDELLESE!

'We couldn't have more excitement if Elvis walked in and asked for a chip sandwich.'

'His eyes are bulging like the belly of a hungry chaffinch.'

'All this cuddling and kissing on stage these days, well it's all right in football when someone scores a goal, but not when you're playing darts.'

DARTS GLOSSARY

Sergeant	used in the game of Rotation, hitting three successive numbers with three darts in a round to win a free turn
Shaft	the portion of the dart that holds the flight
Shanghai	hitting a triple, double, and single of the same number in the same throw
Single In	starting a game without having to hit a double first
Single Out	ending a game without having to hit a double
Spider	the wire assembly which forms the beds on a dartboard
Splashing	throwing two darts at the same time, sometimes with your opposite throwing arm (right handers throw with their left hand), the total points are added up and the player with the highest total goes first. Both darts must hit scoring area of the dartboard or the player throws again.
Sunset Strip	Scoring 77 points in a round

WALKING ON

'Walk this Way' – Aerosmith John Kuczynski
'We are the Champions' – Queen Bobby George
'We Will Rock You' – Queen Phil Nixon
'Wooly Bully' – Terry Jenkins
  Sam the Sham & The Pharaohs

TAYLOR v PRIESTLEY

Dennis Priestley and Phil Taylor have played each other in five World Finals, with Taylor gaining the most victories to date – 4–1.

During the early years of the WDC, Priestley and Taylor had an agreement that they would share prize money won at events – an arrangement that would last between 1994 and 2000. It actually made sense given that generally one or the other (or both) did well in competition. However, the agreement ended with the growth in prize money that enabled players to make good money individually. This period coincided with a sharp dip in form for Dennis.

Taylor and Priestley first met in major competition in the semi-final of the 1990 World Masters. Taylor won that match on his way to the title but Priestley then gained several victories over Taylor in 1991 including the World Championship and British Matchplay final. Other early WDC encounters between the two were won by Priestley. Dennis came out on top in the 1993 UK Matchplay and 1994 World Championship.

Since Taylor's defeat in the 1994 World Final, he has only been defeated on two occasions by Priestley in all competitions and has not suffered a loss on television since 1995.

Despite the intensity of their rivalry, the two of them are still firm friends.

WADDELLESE!

'It's like trying to pin down a kangaroo on a trampoline.'

'They won't just have to play outta their skin to beat Phil Taylor. They'll have to play outta their essence!'

'William Tell could take an apple off your head, Taylor could take out a processed pea.'

'Big Cliff Lazarenko's idea of exercise is sitting in a room with the windows open taking the lid off something cool and fizzy.'

'The atmosphere is so tense, if Elvis walked in with a portion of chips, you could hear the vinegar sizzle on them.'

'If we had Phil Taylor at Hastings in 1066, the Normans would have gone home.'

TAYLOR v PART

Phil Taylor's rivalry with Canadian John Part, who won the BDO World Championship in 1994, began with their first meeting in the 2001 PDC World Championship final. Taylor took the match impressively, 7–0, and he averaged 107.

Taylor was the victor in their first five meetings, but in the 2003 World Championship, Part beat Taylor 7–6 to end Phil's eight-tournament unbeaten run in the championship.

Taylor was also beaten by Part in the 2003 Las Vegas Desert Classic, the 2004 UK Open and at the 2005 World Matchplay.

Part won the 2008 PDC World Championship with a victory over the youngster Kirk Shepherd in the final, and thus is the only man other than Taylor to have won the tournament on more than one occasion. Phil Taylor has not been defeated by Part since the 2005 World Matchplay.

DARTS GLOSSARY

Three in a Bed	throwing all three darts in the same number
Ton	100 points in a round
Ton-Eighty	the highest possible score in a round of darts, scored by hitting three triple 20s in a round
Tops	the double 20
Two and 6	scoring 26 points in a round
Two Fat Ladies	scoring 88 points in a round
Trombones	scoring 66 points in a round

DID YOU KNOW?

James Wade quit his job at a garage in Aldershot twelve days before the World Matchplay 2006, to concentrate on becoming a full-time professional darts player.

DAY JOBS

Over the years, some of the world's most famous darts players have come from a surprising range of employment backgrounds and some professionals continue to work while competing on the circuit.

Here are just a few examples of what some darts players have done, or are still doing:

Gary Anderson	Grate builder
Steve Beaton	Driving instructor
Eric Bristow	MFI/advertising agency
Brendan Dolan	Painter and decorator
Bobby George	Bouncer/window cleaner/floor layer/ tunnel digger (Victoria Line)/ plasterer
Trina Gulliver	Joiner
Rod Harrington	Roofer/professional footballer
Mark Hylton	Airline cabin crew
Terry Jenkins	Antiques dealer
Cliff Lazarenko	Labourer
Colin Lloyd	Builder
John Lowe	Carpenter
Peter Manley	Newsagent
Wayne Mardle	Accountant
Kevin Painter	Ground Worker
Andy Smith	Tree Surgeon
Co Stompé	Tram driver
Phil Taylor	Maker of ceramic toilet chain handles/sheet metal worker
Ray Barneveld	Postman
James Wade	Car mechanic
Robert Wagner	Bodybuilder
Mark Webster	Plumber

| Simon Whitlock | Bricklayer |
| Jocky Wilson | Miner/paint factory worker/chef |

WADDELLESE!

'Jocky Wilson . . . What an athlete!'

'Look at the man go, it's like trying to stop a water buffalo with a pea-shooter!'
Sid describes how it must feel to play Phil Taylor

'The atmosphere is a cross between the Munich Beer Festival and the Coliseum when the Christians were on the menu!'

'This lad has more checkouts than Tescos!'

DID YOU KNOW?

At 25 years old Adrian Lewis, on winning the PDC World Championship in 2011, became the fifth youngest player to win a World Championship. He fell behind Jelle Klaasen (who was 21 when he won in 2006), Eric Bristow (22 in 1980), Keith Deller (23 in 1983), and Mark Webster (24 in 2008). Lewis was also the youngest ever PDC World Champion. Lewis's run to the final was the first time in PDC history that a player had reached the World Championship final having never played full-time on the BDO circuit. Before that year, only four different players had won the PDC version of the World Championship, and all of them were former winners of the rival British Darts Organisation Championship.

DARTS GLOSSARY

Upstairs	the upper section of the board
Wiring	bouncing a dart off a wire

THE SID AND FRY SHOW

On a Monday evening in May 2010 actor, writer and comedian Stephen Fry joined Sid Waddell and Rod Harrington in the Sky Sports commentary box. Fry, a huge darts fan, covered the semi-final clash in the Premier League Darts between Phil Taylor and Mervyn King.

The event had been postponed from the day before owing to a power cut, but Fry's love of darts caused him to reorganise his busy schedule to allow him to make his date with Sid and Rod. Stephen spent time in the players' room where Mervyn King explained his darts to him and he and Phil Taylor shared jokes, while James Wade wanted a photo with Fry for his mum.

As those familiar with Fry's work (and who isn't?) might have expected, he coped admirably with the commentary, squashed up tight to Waddell, with Sid flaying dangerously about as the heat of the battle inspired him to his usual physical animation; this was television history in the making. Stephen demonstrated his deep knowledge of the game and even managed to identify some of the finishes before spotter Keith Deller.

Following Taylor's dismissal of King, Waddell waxed nostalgic, mourning, 'Once upon a time he was breaking all records . . . Now he's only breaking Merv's heart. Nothing you can do – a total eclipse of the darts.'

Fry chipped in wistfully, 'Ahhh . . . Bonnie Tyler,' crediting the gravel-edge-voiced Princess of Welsh of rock-pop who, decades previously, when Waddell was no more than a slip of a lad, had ground out the source of Sid's rumination to popular acclaim.

'Taylor could hit the dandruff on a fly's forelock,' Sid continued. Fry took his lead, 'I'm like a pig in Chardonnay.'

WHAT THEY SAID

'If you hold your throw, you never know.'

John Gwynne

'Who let the dogs out?'

The Lakeside crowd after a streaker got on the oche in 2001 as Ted Hankey played Shaun Greatbach

'I won my fair share, I but wanted more.'

Peter Manley talking of how as a teenager he often played for money

DID YOU KNOW?

Phil Taylor has an infrared sauna at his home to help him acclimatise to the hot stage lights.

FOR THE RECORD

In March 1987, Jocky Wilson threw a 24-dart 1,001 leg against American Bud Trumbower in at the Eastgate US marine base. His scores were: 180, 140, 140, 140, 81, 100, 120 (out). Jocky scored a terrific 600 points with his first 12 darts and doubled out with treble 20-20-double 20 to come away with a 41.7 per-dart average.

WORLD CHAMPIONSHIPS – WHO WON WHAT & WHEN?

British Darts Organisation World Championships

Year	Winner	Score	Runner-Up
1978	Leighton Rees	11–7	John Lowe
1979	John Lowe	5–0	Leighton Rees
1980	Eric Bristow	5–3	Bobby George
1981	Eric Bristow	5–3	John Lowe
1982	Jocky Wilson	5–3	John Lowe
1983	Keith Deller	6–5	Eric Bristow
1984	Eric Bristow	7–1	Dave Whitcombe
1985	Eric Bristow	6–2	John Lowe
1986	Eric Bristow	6–0	Dave Whitcombe
1987	John Lowe	6–4	Eric Bristow
1988	Bob Anderson	6–4	John Lowe
1989	Jocky Wilson	6–4	Eric Bristow
1990	Phil Taylor	6–1	Eric Bristow
1991	Dennis Priestley	6–0	Eric Bristow
1992	Phil Taylor	6–5	Mike Gregory

Year	Winner	Score	Runner-Up
1993	John Lowe	6–3	Alan Warriner-Little
1994	John Part	6–0	Bobby George
1995	Richie Burnett	6–3	Raymond van Barneveld
1996	Steve Beaton	6–3	Richie Burnett
1997	Les Wallace	6–3	Marshall James
1998	Raymond van Barneveld	6–5	Richie Burnett
1999	Raymond van Barneveld	6–5	Ronnie Baxter
2000	Ted Hankey	6–0	Ronnie Baxter
2001	John Walton	6–2	Ted Hankey
2002	Tony David	6–4	Mervyn King
2003	Raymond van Barneveld	6–3	Ritchie Davies
2004	Andy Fordham	6–3	Mervyn King
2005	Raymond van Barneveld	6–2	Martin Adams
2006	Jelle Klaasen	7–5	Raymond van Barneveld
2007	Martin Adams	7–6	Phil Nixon
2008	Mark Webster	7–5	Simon Whitlock
2009	Ted Hankey	7–6	Tony O'Shea
2010	Martin Adams	7–5	Dave Chisnall
2011	Martin Adams	7–5	Dean Winstanley

Professional Darts Corporation World Championships

Year	Winner	Score	Runner-Up
1994	Dennis Priestley	6–1	Phil Taylor
1995	Phil Taylor	6–2	Rod Harrington
1996	Phil Taylor	6–4	Dennis Priestley
1997	Phil Taylor	6–3	Dennis Priestley
1998	Phil Taylor	6–0	Dennis Priestley
1999	Phil Taylor	6–2	Peter Manley
2000	Phil Taylor	7–3	Dennis Priestley
2001	Phil Taylor	7–0	John Part
2002	Phil Taylor	7–0	Peter Manley
2003	John Part	7–6	Phil Taylor
2004	Phil Taylor	7–6	Kevin Painter
2005	Phil Taylor	7–4	Mark Dudbridge
2006	Phil Taylor	7–0	Peter Manley
2007	Raymond van Barneveld	7–6	Phil Taylor
2008	John Part	7–2	Kirk Shepherd
2009	Phil Taylor	7–1	Raymond van Barneveld
2010	Phil Taylor	7–3	Simon Whitlock
2011	Adrian Lewis	7–5	Gary Anderson

THE TWO WORLD CUPS OF DARTS

The WDF World Cup has been held every other year since 1977. There are team, pair and singles events within the championships. If you fancy going along, the next World Cup event is scheduled to take place in Canada in 2013.

Year	Winners	Team	Singles	Pairs
1977	Wales	Leighton Rees Alan Evans David Jones (Wales)	Leighton Rees (Wales)	Eric Bristow John Lowe (England)
1979	England	Eric Bristow John Lowe Tony Brown Bill Lennard (England)	Nicky Virachkul (USA)	Eric Bristow John Lowe (England)
1981	England	Eric Bristow John Lowe Tony Brown Cliff Lazarenko (England)	John Lowe (England)	Cliff Lazarenko Tony Brown (England)
1983	England	Eric Bristow John Lowe Keith Deller Dave Whitcombe (England)	Eric Bristow (England)	Eric Bristow John Lowe (England)
1985	England	Tony Payne Rick Ney John Kramer Dan Valletto (USA)	Eric Bristow (England)	Eric Bristow John Lowe (England)
1987	England	Eric Bristow John Lowe Cliff Lazarenko Bob Anderson (England)	Eric Bristow (England)	Eric Bristow John Lowe (England)

Year	Winners	Team	Singles	Pairs
1989	England	Bob Sinnaeve Rick Bisaro Tony Holyoake Albert Anstey (Canada)	Eric Bristow (England)	Eric Bristow John Lowe (England)
1991	England	Eric Bristow John Lowe Phil Taylor Alan Warriner-Little (England)	John Lowe (England)	Keith Sullivan Wayne Weening (Australia)
1993	Wales	Steve Beaton Ronnie Baxter Kevin Kenny Dave Askew (England)	Roland Scholten (Netherlands)	John Part Carl Mercer (Canada)
1995	England	Steve Beaton Ronnie Baxter Martin Adams Andy Fordham (England)	Martin Adams (England)	Martin Adams Andy Fordham (England)
1997	Wales	Eric Burden Marshall James Sean Palfrey Martin Phillips (Wales)	Raymond van Barneveld (Netherlands)	Sean Palfrey Martin Phillips (Wales)

Year	Winners	Team	Singles	Pairs
1999	England	Ronnie Baxter Martin Adams Andy Fordham Mervyn King (England)	Raymond van Barneveld (Netherlands)	Ritchie Davies Richie Herbert (Wales)
2001	England	Martin Adams Andy Fordham Mervyn King John Walton (England)	Martin Adams (England)	Andy Fordham John Walton (England)
2003	England	Ray Carver John Kuczynski Bill Davis George Walls (USA)	Raymond van Barneveld (Netherlands)	Martin Adams Mervyn King (England)
2005	Netherlands	Jarkko Komula Ulf Ceder Marko Pusa Kim Viljanen (Finland)	Dick van Dijk (Netherlands)	Raymond van Barneveld Vincent van der Voort (Netherlands)
2007	Netherlands	Martin Adams Steve Farmer Tony O'Shea John Walton (England)	Mark Webster (Wales)	Mario Robbe Joey ten Berge (Netherlands)

Year	Winners	Team	Singles	Pairs
2009	Netherlands	Joey ten Berge Willy van de Wiel Frans Harmsen Daniel Brouwer (Netherlands)	Tony O'Shea (England)	Anthony Fleet Geoff Kime (Australia)
2011	England	Scott Waites Tony O'Shea Martin Atkins Martin Adams (England)	Scott Waites (England)	Tony O'Shea Martin Adams (England)

In October 2009, Barry Hearn, Chairman of the PDC, offered to buy the BDO in order to give the amateur sport a £2 million boost. The BDO declined Hearn's offer.

Following the BDO's rejection, the PDC announced three new tournaments for 2010, one of which was the PDC World Cup of Darts.

The inaugural PDC World Cup of Darts took place at the Rainton Meadows Arena in Houghton-le-Spring over several snowy days in December 2010. The heavily fancied English pair of Wade and Taylor had their World Cup hopes dashed early on by the relatively unknown Spanish duo of Alcinas and Rodriguez in the second round of the tournament. In the final Wales met the Netherlands. In a fantastically entertaining match, Co Stompé and Raymond van Barneveld triumphed over the brave Welsh pair of Barrie Bates and Mark Webster, both of whom had played some scintillating darts over the course of the tournament.

2010	Netherlands	4–2	Wales
	Co Stompé		Barrie Bates
	Raymond van Barneveld		Mark Webster